# To Speak in Your Presence

### A treasury of personal prayer

## Kevin Mayhew

*For Barbara, with love.*

First published in 1995 by
KEVIN MAYHEW LTD
Rattlesden
Bury St Edmunds
Suffolk IP30 0SZ

© 1995 Kevin Mayhew Ltd

ISBN  8 86209 651 0
Catalogue No  1500028

Front cover: *St. Dorothy*, 1904, by Edward Reginald Frampton
(1872-1923). Reproduced by kind permission of the
Maas Gallery, London/Bridgeman Art Library, London.
Cover design by Graham Johnstone

Typesetting and Page Creation by Vicky Brown
Printed and bound in Great Britain.

# Foreword

This collection of prayers, like many others, I imagine, began life to meet a personal need for a vade-mecum.

Although I have chosen these particular prayers because I like them and each one speaks to me, I hope they will also commend themselves to others. *To Speak in Your Presence* is not comprehensive: there are gaps which, in spite of extensive reading and research, I have been unable to fill. I have avoided the route of commissioning specific new material for this purpose because experience indicates that the most effective prayers come from a deep need rather than a passing request.

Most of the prayers are given in the singular form as befits a book of personal devotion. Archaic words which have lost their meaning have been revised and inclusive language is used throughout. Living authors and the literary trustees of those authors still in copyright have been willing without exception to allow these revisions. It is my earnest hope that those who use *To Speak in Your Presence* will feel that these emendations have been done with skill and sensitivity and are true to the wishes of the original authors.

Recorded prayer comes to us from pre-Christian times and there are, of course, Biblical prayers, which is where this book starts, continuing through two thousand years to our own time. There are new prayers in *To Speak in Your Presence,* mostly by friends whose work I have known over many years. I hope a short roll call of some of these outstanding contributions will not embarrass their authors when I mention, with gratitude, Alan Rees, Titular Abbot of Tewkesbury, Graham Jeffery, rector of Thakeham, and the nuns of the Carmelite Monastery, Quidenham. I thank also Robert Van de Weyer, pastor of the Society of Christ the Sower at Little Gidding, Cambridgeshire, whose *Fount Book of Prayer* has provided much inspiration and valuable material. Katherine Laidler has given me invaluable assistance, I am most grateful to her.

In compiling *To Speak in Your Presence* I have become increasingly aware of my own shortcomings, both in the realms of theology, and as an editor. However, I was fortunate to be able to call on the great talent and generous nature of Michael Forster who has not only advised me throughout but also revised many of the older prayers to reflect a truly resurrection-based Christianity. The aim of this book is a positive one – not to lead us through pious gloom to a greater awareness of guilt and sin, but to enable God to reach us with a grace which overrules our weakness, stands us on our feet and makes us glad to serve and praise him.

KEVIN MAYHEW

# Contents

# Prayers of Invocation

As the sun rises, Lord,                                           *1*
    let your light shine on me.
    Destroy the darkness about me,
    scatter the darkness before me,
    disperse the darkness behind me,
    dispel the darkness within me.
Let your light shine on me.

As the sun rises, Lord,
    let your light shine on me;
    the warmth of your presence,
    the brightness of your love,
    the radiance of your joy,
    the shining of your hope.
Let your light shine on me.

As the sun rises, Lord,
    let your light shine on me;
    your light to guide,
    your light to lead,
    your light to direct,
    your light to brighten.
Let your light shine on me.

*David Adam*

Come, Holy Spirit, fill my heart                                  *2*
    and enkindle within it the fire of your love.
Send forth your Spirit,
    to re-create my heart and renew your creation.
As you have taught all your people by the light of the Holy Spirit,
    grant that by the gift of the same Spirit I may find wisdom,
    and always rejoice in his consolation.

*Author unknown*

3    Dear Lord, help me to remove from my mind
      every thought or opinion
      which you would not sanction,
      every feeling from my heart
      which you would not approve.
   Grant that I may spend the hours of the day
      gladly working with you according to your will.
   Help me just for today, and be with me in it:
      in the long hours of work,
      that I may not grow weary or slack in serving you;
      in conversations,
      that they may not be to me occasions of uncharitableness;
      in the day's worries and disappointments,
      that I may be patient with myself and with those around me;
      in moments of fatigue and illness,
      that I may be mindful of others' feelings
      rather than of my own.
   Be with me in times of temptation,
      that I may be generous and loyal,
      so that when the day is over
      I may lay it at your feet,
      with its successes which glorify you,
      and its failures which remind me of my weakness,
      and feel that life is real and peaceful,
      and blessed when spent with you as the guest of my soul.

*Traditional*

4    O Christ, deep water of joy,
      I long to drink from you!
   Come, Lord, in your eager love:
      free me from my sinfulness;
      fill me with your praise;
      and I will sing your glory.

*Carmelite Monastery, Quidenham*

Holy Spirit, Lord and giver of life, be present.   5
 In my weakness, be my strength;
 in my tiredness, be my freshness;
 in my dirtiness, be my cleansing;
 in my blindness, be my vision;
 in my coldness, be my fervour;
 in my meanness, be my generosity;
 in my hard-heartedness, be my gentle compassion;
 in my stupidity, be my clarity;
 in my arrogance, be my humility;
 in my complexity, be my simplicity;
 in my anxiety, be my peace;
 in my hurt, be my healing;
 in my suffering, be my consolation;
 in my troubles, be my calm;
 in my doubts and despondency, be my hope;
 in my sin, be my forgiveness, mercy and salvation;
for the sake of Jesus and the glory of the Father.

*Alan Rees OSB (b. 1941)*

Soul of Christ, sanctify me.   6
Body of Christ, fill me.
Blood of Christ, save me.
Water from the side of Christ, wash me.
Passion of Jesus, strengthen me.
O good Jesus, hear me.
Let me not be separated from you.
From the malicious enemy defend me.
In the hour of my death, call me,
 and bid me come to you,
that with your saints I may praise you
 for ever and ever.

*Pope John XXII (1249-1334)*

7   At those times, Lord, when I feel alone, adrift,
    a solitary someone in a crowded world,
    you come and gently touch me
    to remind me that you care;
        through answered prayer,
        or the smile of a friend,
        a promise kept or a gift of kindness;
        with a rainbow or one perfect rose;
        with an unexpected letter from
        someone who is thinking of me.
    These are the moments when I catch a shining
        glimpse of the ways you share your love.

*Author unknown*

8   You possess me, Lord,
        and I possess you.
    You have put your faith and hope in me,
        and I have put my faith and hope in you.
    My life, my honour,
        my happiness, my peace,
        all rest on you.
    You can see every second of my life;
        let me see you.
    I pray that you will grant me a single moment
        when I can look at you face to face.
    Then I will be able to give you all my heart,
        all my love.
    Do not wait until I have died,
        but let me see you even here on earth.
    I know that I have no right to ask this favour
        because my heart is so lukewarm,
        so indifferent.
    Make me worthy of such a privilege;
        make my heart ready to receive you,
        and my soul ready to see you.

*Simeon the Theodidact (c. 949-1022)*

God of the still, small voice,     9
   let my spirit today stay far from loneliness.
Let me, instead,
   discover the richness found in solitude,
   appreciate the quiet times for prayer and private reflection,
   and feel contentment and comfort in my aloneness.
Yet, if my thoughts should turn to loneliness today,
   as they sometimes do,
   let me find the strength to reach out to
   others for companionship,
   support and understanding.
Let me give thanks for the happy parts of my life,
   accept the lonely times as a natural part of living,
   and change what needs changing
   so that I may find peace of mind and gladness of heart.
Lord, help me to remember that I am never truly alone,
   for you are always here with me.

*Author unknown*


Shine into our hearts, O Christ,     10
   with the pure light of your clear knowledge of God,
   and open the eyes of our minds to your teaching,
   for you are the light of our souls and of our whole selves,
   O Christ our friend and our God.

*Martin Shaw*


With all my heart, O Lord,     11
I long for you:
Fulfil my loving, longing hope.
Take me in your arms
   and keep me safe.

*Carmelite Monastery, Quidenham*

12    Lord, this is your feast,
        prepared by your longing,
        spread at your command,
        attended at your invitation,
        blessed by your own word,
        offered by your own hand,
        the undying memorial of your sacrifice upon the cross,
        the full gift of your everlasting love,
        and its perpetuation until time shall end.
Lord, this is bread of heaven, bread of life:
        whoever eats it will hunger no more.
And this is the cup of pardon, healing, gladness, strength:
        whoever drinks it will never thirst again.
So may we come, O Lord, to your table;
        Lord Jesus, come to us.

*Eric Milner-White (1884-1964)*

13    Help me, Lord,
        always to wait for you,
        to wish for you
        and to watch for you,
        so that at your coming you may find me ready.
For your sake I ask it.

*Author unknown*

14    Show me your face,
        O Lord, unseen King,
        that my joy may be complete.
Living with you
        I shall become like you.

*Carmelite Monastery, Quidenham*

Eternal Light, shine into my heart,                                    15
Eternal Goodness, deliver me from evil,
Eternal Power, be my support,
Eternal Wisdom, scatter the darkness of my ignorance,
Eternal Pity, have mercy upon me,
    that with all my heart and mind
    and soul and strength
    I may seek your face
    and be brought by your infinite mercy
    to your holy presence,
    through Jesus Christ my Lord.

*Alcuin of York (c. 735-804)*


Spirit of God,                                                         16
    powerful and unpredictable as the wind,
    you came upon the followers of Jesus at Pentecost
    and swept them off their feet,
    so that they found themselves doing
    what they thought they never had it in them to do.
    It is you who, through all ages,
    have fired people with enthusiasm
    to go about telling the good news of Jesus
    and serving other people for his sake.
Spirit of God,
    powerful and unpredictable as the wind,
    come upon me as I worship
    and become the driving force of my life.

*From Contemporary Prayers*


O heavenly King, Comforter, Spirit of truth,                          17
    you are found in every place and fill all things,
    source of abundant blessings and giver of life.
Come and live in me,
    cleanse me from all impurity,
    and by your goodness fit me for eternal life.

*Eastern Orthodox*

18    Stay with me, Lord Jesus,
        so that I shall begin to shine as you shine,
        as a light to others.
    The light will be all from you.
    It will be you who shine through me upon others.
    Give light to them as well as to me;
        light them with me, through me.
    Help me witness to you without preaching;
        not by words but by example
        and by the sympathetic influence of what I do;
        by my visible resemblance to your saints
        and the evident fullness of my love for you.

*John Henry Newman (1801-1890)*

19    Lord, you humble yourself.
    You bow down like a servant.
    You give yourself always for me.
    Teach me to learn from you
        how to love,
        how to hold nothing back,
        how to give myself.
    Fill me with your Spirit,
        that Spirit of loving and serving
        all our brothers and sisters sincerely,
        without counting the cost.

*Liturgical Institute, Trier*

20    Lord, put your hands on my eyes,
        that I shall be able to see not only
        that which is visible
        but also that which is invisible.
    Let my eyes be focused not only on
        that which is present
        but also on that which is to come.
    Unseal my heart's visions,
        that I may gaze on you in your glory.

*Origen (c. 185-254)*

I pray, Lord, that everything I do 21
    may be prompted by your inspiration,
    so that every prayer and work of mine
    may begin from you
    and be brought by you to completion.

*Based on the Prologue of St. Benedict's Rule*

Lord Jesus Christ, pierce my soul with your love 22
    so that I may always long for you alone,
    who are the bread of angels
    and the fulfilment of the soul's deepest desires.
May my heart always hunger and feed upon you,
so that my soul may be filled with the
    sweetness of your presence.
May my soul thirst for you,
    who are the source of life,
    wisdom, knowledge, light
    and all the riches of God our Father.
May I always seek and find you,
    think upon you,
    speak to you
    and do all things for the honour
    and glory of your holy name.
Be always my only hope,
    my peace, my refuge and my help
    in whom my heart is rooted
    so that I may never be separated from you.

*St Bonaventure (1221-1274)*

In me, my God, be present, 23
    be always here.
And may you find your home in me,
    just as you are, my God.

*Carmelite Monastery, Quidenham*

Come, Lord Jesus, come. 24

# Prayers
# for Grace

Take away from me, O God,                                    *25*
    all pride and vanity,
    all boasting and forwardness,
and give me the true courage
    that shows itself by gentleness;
the true wisdom
    that shows itself by simplicity;
and the true power
    that shows itself by modesty.

                              *Charles Kingsley (1819-1875)*


Jesus, Master Carpenter of Nazareth,                         *26*
    who on the cross through wood and nails
    worked our whole salvation,
    wield well your tools in this your workshop that I,
    who come to you rough-hewn,
    may by your hand be fashioned to a truer beauty
    and a greater usefulness,
    for the honour of your name.

                                        *Toc H Prayer*


My Father in heaven,                                         *27*
teach me the value of little things.
Show me how to consecrate what seems insignificant,
and to recognise the light of your presence in every moment.
May I glorify the day by offering
each minute to be redeemed by your love.
I offer you all my moments.

                              *J. H. Jowett (1864-1923)*

28 Almighty and ever-living God,
I approach the sacrament of your only-begotten Son,
   the Lord Jesus Christ.
I come sick to the doctor of life,
   unclean to the fountain of mercy,
   sightless to the radiance of eternal light,
   poor and needy to the Lord of heaven and earth.
Lord, in your great generosity,
   heal my sickness,
   wash away my defilement,
   enlighten my blindness,
   enrich my poverty,
   and clothe my nakedness.
May I receive the bread of angels,
   the King of kings and Lord of lords,
   with humble reverence,
   with purity and faith,
   with the repentance and love
   and with the determined purpose
   that will help to bring me to salvation.
May I receive the sacrament of the Lord's body and blood,
   and its reality and power.
Kind God,
   may I receive the body of your only begotten Son,
   the Lord Jesus Christ,
   born from the womb of the virgin Mary,
   and so be received into his mystical body
   and numbered among the members of his church.
Loving Father,
   as on my earthly pilgrimage
   I now receive your beloved Son
   under the veil of a sacrament,
   may I one day see him face to face in glory,
   who lives and reigns with you for ever.

*St. Thomas Aquinas (c.1225-1274)*

Grant, O Lord, 29
    that I may not set my heart on earthly things,
    but love the things of heaven.
And help me now,
    while I am placed among things that are passing away,
    to cling to those that will last for ever,
    through Jesus Christ my Lord.

*Leonine Sacramentary (5th Century)*

O God my Father, I give you thanks 30
    that today you are calling me to worship you
    and to learn of you.
You know the needs with which I will go to your house.
Grant that in it I may find comfort for sorrow,
    and soothing for soreness of heart.
Grant that in it I may find guidance for problems
    and light for perplexity of mind.
Grant that in it I may find strength against my temptations
    and grace to overcome the fascination of the wrong things.
Grant that in it I may meet Jesus,
    and go out not to forget him any more.
Remember those who cannot go to church today:
    those who are ill;
    those who are aged;
    those who are too sad to come;
    those who have the care of children
    and of family concerns;
    those who are nursing invalids;
    those who must work even today.
And grant that in their own home,
    in the hospitals,
    the infirmaries,
    the nursing homes,
    they may know the unseen fellowship
    of the worshipping company
    of those who love you.

*William Barclay (1907-1978)*

31    O God my Father, direct and control me in every part of my life:
      my tongue, that I speak no false words;
      my actions, that I may do nothing to shame myself
      or hurt others;
      my mind, that I may think no evil or bitter thoughts;
      my heart, that it may be set only on pleasing you.

*Catholic Prayer Book*

32    O Lord,
      support me all through the long day of my life,
      until the shadows lengthen
      and the evening comes,
      and the busy world is hushed,
      and the fever of life over,
      and my work is done.
Then, Lord, in your mercy,
      grant me a safe lodging,
      a holy rest,
      and peace at the last.

*John Henry Newman (1801-1890)*

33    Almighty God,
to you all hearts are open and all desires known,
and from you no secrets are hidden:
      cleanse the thoughts of my heart
      by the inspiration of your Holy Spirit,
      that I may perfectly love you
      and worthily praise your holy name.

*Author unknown*

Lord, you know better than I know myself that 34
    I am growing older
    and will someday be old.
Keep me from the fatal habit of thinking I must say something
    on every subject and on every occasion.

Release me from craving to straighten out everybody's affairs.
Make me thoughtful but not moody;
    helpful but not bossy.
With my vast store of wisdom,
    it seems a pity not to use it all,
    but you know, Lord,
    that I want a few friends at the end.

Keep my mind free from the recital of endless details;
    give me wings to get to the point.
Seal my lips on my aches and pains;
    they are increasing,
    and love of rehearsing them
    is becoming sweeter as the years go be.
I dare not ask for grace enough to enjoy
    the tales of others' pains,
    but help me to endure them with patience.

I dare not ask for improved memory,
    but for a growing humility and a lessening cocksureness
    when my memory seems to clash with the memories of others.
Teach me the glorious lesson that occasionally
    I may be mistaken.

Keep me reasonably sweet.
I do not want to be a saint
    – some of them are so hard to live with –
    but a sour old person is no great companion, either.

Give me the ability to see good things in unexpected places,
    and talents in unexpected people.
And give me, O Lord, the grace to tell them so.

*Seventeenth Century Nun's Prayer*

35  Thank you, Lord, for this brand new day.
    Give me the wisdom to see its possibilities,
        the strength to face its challenges,
        and the grace to be open to its promise.
    Give me your heart of love to do a favour,
        speak a kindness, offer a hand,
        soothe a hurt, celebrate a joy,
        share a sorrow, or in some small way
        give of myself in love to another
        in your name.

*Author unknown*


36  Guard my eyes, O Lord,
        so that seeing other people's wealth
        will not make me covetous.
    Guard my ears,
        so that they will not listen to foolish
        and malicious gossip.
    Guard my heart,
        so that I shall not take pleasure
        in the temptations of the world.
    Guard my hands,
        so that they will not be used for violence
        or for exploiting others.
    Guard my feet upon the gentle earth,
        so that in the bustle of life
        I shall not forget the value of rest.

*Based on a traditional Irish prayer*


37  God give me work
        till my life shall end
    and life
        till my work is done.

*Epitaph of Winifred Holtby (1898-1935)*

Lord, I believe in you:
   increase my faith.
I trust in you:
   strengthen my trust.
I love you:
   let me love you more and more.
I am sorry for my sins:
   deepen my repentance.

I worship you
   as my first beginning,
I long for you
   as my last end.
I praise you
   as my constant helper,
and call on you
   as my loving protector.

38

*Author unknown*

Gracious and holy Father,
   give me wisdom to recognise you,
   intelligence to understand you,
   diligence to seek you,
   patience to wait for you,
   eyes to see you,
   a heart to meditate on you,
   and life to proclaim you,
   through the power of the Spirit of Jesus Christ my Lord.

39

*St. Benedict (c.480-547)*

God grant me
   the serenity to accept the things I cannot change,
   the courage to change the things I can,
   and wisdom to know the difference.

40

*Author unknown*

41  Teach me, Lord, to hope in you,
     for you are the source and fount of all creation.
Open my heart to know you
     who alone are the highest and most holy.
Grant me, Lord, your help and protection.
     Save the afflicted, raise the fallen,
     reveal yourself to the needy, heal the sick,
     and bring home your wandering people.
     Feed the hungry, set free the captive,
     support the weak, comfort the faint-hearted.
Most merciful Lord,
     forgive me my sins and offences,
     my errors and shortcomings.
     Do not hold my sin against me,
     but make me clean.
Guide me in all that I do,
     so that I may walk in holiness of heart,
     and my actions may be pleasing in your sight.
Show me the light of your face in peace;
     shelter me by your mighty hand,
     and save me from all wrongdoing by your outstretched arm.
Give to me, and to all people, peace and harmony.
     Make me obedient to your almighty and glorious name
     and give me a proper regard for those in authority on earth.
     Grant to them health, peace and security,
     that they may exercise, and not abuse
     whatever authority you have given them.
To you, who alone can supply these and all good things,
     I offer my praises through Jesus Christ,
     the high priest and guardian of my soul.
Through him be glory and majesty to you
     now and for all generations through all ages.

*St. Clement of Rome (d. c.100)*

Lord God, 42
　the light of the minds that know you,
　the life of the souls that love you,
　and the strength of the wills that serve you:
　help me so to know you that I may truly love you,
　and so to love you that I may fully serve you,
　whom to serve is perfect freedom.

*St. Augustine of Hippo (354-430)*

Grant me, Lord, to know what I ought to know, 43
　to love what I ought to love,
　to praise what delights you most,
　to value what is precious in your sight,
　and to hate what is offensive to you.
Let me not judge according to superficial appearances,
nor condemn on the basis of what others say;
but may I have the discernment to understand deeper realities,
and above all things to seek your will.

*Thomas à Kempis (c.1380-1471)*

Holy Lord, teach me the meaning of real success, 44
　and let me not become enslaved by the values of the world,
　but value holiness more than wealth.
May I aspire to what is eternal,
　and in that may I be successful!

*J. H. Jowett (1864-1923)*

45  Grant, O Lord, that the hands that have taken holy things
        may daily bring forth fruit to your glory.
    Grant, O Lord, that the lips which have sung your
        praise within the sanctuary
        may glorify you for ever;
        that the ears which have heard the music of your songs
        may be closed to clamour and dispute;
        that the eyes which have seen your great love
        may also see your blessed hope;
        that the tongues which have sung the Sanctus
        may ever speak the truth.
    Grant that the feet which have trod in your holy place
        may always walk in the light,
        and that the souls and bodies which have tasted
        of your body and blood
        may ever be restored in newness of life.

*Liturgy of Malabar*


46  O God, make the door of this house
        wide enough to receive all who need
        human love and fellowship,
        and a heavenly Father's care,
        and narrow enough to shut out all envy,
        pride and hate.
    Make its threshold smooth enough to be no
        stumbling block to children,
        nor to straying feet,
        but rugged enough to turn back the tempter's power.
    Make it a gateway to your eternal kingdom.

*Thomas Ken (1637-1711)*

Bless me, O Lord God, with all heavenly grace,     47
    and make me pure and holy in your sight.
May the riches of your glory abound in me;
    instruct me with the word of truth,
    inform me with the gospel of salvation,
    and enrich me in your love.

*Gelasian Sacramentary (6th Century)*

O my God, I offer you all my thoughts,     48
    words, actions and sufferings;
and I pray that you will give me your grace
    that I may not offend you this day,
    but may faithfully serve you
    and do your holy will in all things.

*Traditional*

Give me a sense of humour, Lord,     49
    and also things to laugh about.
Give me the grace to take a joke against myself
    and see the funny side of the things I do.
Save me from annoyance,
    bad temper,
    resentment against my friends.
Help me to laugh even in the face of trouble.
Fill my mind with the love of Jesus,
    for his name's sake.

*A. G. Bullivant*

50  Lord, help me to remember that all time belongs to you,
        and that I am responsible to you for my use of it.
    Help me neither to waste time
        nor to be so obsessed with saving it
        that I become the slave of time
        and lose my sense of proportion and values.
    Lord, teach me to use my time to your glory:
        creatively,
        re-creatively,
        in that rhythm of involvement in the world
        and of withdrawal from the world
        which is your will for me.
    Save me both from running away from the world
        into self-centred religiosity
        and from running away from the inner life
        into compulsive busyness.
    Lord, help me to live each day
        so that at the end of it
        there is nothing I cannot share with you,
        nothing for which I cannot thank you.

*Margaret Dewey (b. 1923)*

51  Lord Jesus, my Saviour,
        let me now come to you.
    My heart is cold:
        warm it by your selfless love.
    My heart is sinful:
        cleanse it by your precious blood.
    My heart is weak:
        strengthen it by your joyous Spirit
    My heart is empty:
        fill it with your divine presence.
    Lord Jesus, my heart is yours:
        possess it always and only for yourself.

*St. Augustine of Hippo (354-430)*

My Father, teach me the spirit of true worship.     *52*
Save me from unnecessary formality,
and from becoming enslaved to tradition for its own sake.
Let my approach to you be at once reverent and joyful,
and my fellowship with your people both holy and satisfying.

*J. H. Jowett (1864-1923)*


O Lord my God,     *53*
    teach my heart this day
    where and how to see you,
    where and how to find you.
You have made and remade me,
    and you have given to me
    all the truly good things I possess,
    and still I do not know you.
I have not yet done that for which I was created.
Teach me to seek you,
    for I cannot seek you unless you teach me,
    or find you unless you show yourself to me.
Let me seek you in my longing,
    let me long for you in my seeking.
Let me find you by loving you,
    let me love you when I find you.

*St. Anselm (1033-1109)*


This is my prayer to you, O Lord:     *54*
    Give me the strength to bear my joys and sorrows lightly;
    give me the strength to make my love fruitful in service;
    give me the strength never to disown the poor
    or bow before the abuse of power.
    give me the strength to raise my mind high above petty things,
    and give me the strength lovingly
    to surrender my strength to your will.

*Rabindranath Tagore (1862-1941)*

*When the master of ceremonies tasted the water that had been turned into wine, he said: 'You have kept the best wine until now.' (John 2:9-10)*

55    I do not ask to be filled with wine, Lord.
Ordinary water will be enough.
Though I long sometimes for a more visible discipleship,
    a more obvious way of serving you.
And yet,
    being filled with this plain water, Lord,
    I only ask that you pass
    your hand over it,
    changing its contents,
    with all their inadequacy,
    into your wine.

*Graham Jeffery (b. 1935)*

56    Father,
you have given to me so very many gifts.
May I profit by them to grow in your truth.
For I want to be one of those
    who will come into your presence,
    who will share your dwelling place
    at the end of time.

*Carmelite Monastery, Quidenham*

57    I ask for daily bread, but not for wealth
    lest I forget the poor.
I ask for strength, but not for power
    lest I despise the meek.
I ask for wisdom, but not for learning
    lest I despise the simple.
I ask for good repute, but not for fame
    lest I demean the lowly.
I ask for peace of mind, but not for idle hours
    lest I fail to respond to the call of duty.

*Inazo Nitobe*

You, Lord, are the bread of life      *58*
   and the well of holiness.

Just as you feed me day by day
   with the food that sustains my body,
   keeping me alive on earth,
   I pray that you will feed my soul
   with the spiritual bread of eternity,
   making me ready for heaven.

Just as you satisfy my bodily thirst
   with cool water from the rivers and streams,
   I pray that you will pour the waters
   of holiness into my soul,
   making my every work and action
   a joyful sign of your love.

*St. Basil of Caesarea (c.330-379)*

How good you are, Lord,      *59*
and how near to me
– so near that I may always talk to you,
   be comforted by you,
   breathe through you,
   be enlightened by you,
   find peace in you,
   and gain spiritual nourishment from you.
Grant that my fellowship with you
   may never be polluted by malice,
   pride, envy, greed,
   gluttony or falsehood.
Grant that I may belong wholly to you.

*John Sergieff (1829-1908)*

60 Eternal Father of my soul,
 let my first thought today be of you;
 let my first impulse be to worship you;
 let my first speech be your name;
 let my first action be to kneel before you in prayer.

For your perfect wisdom and goodness;
 for the love which you have for all creation;
 for the love which you have for me;
 for the great opportunity of my life;
 for the indwelling of your Spirit in my heart;
 for the sevenfold gifts of your Spirit,
 I praise and worship you, O Lord.

Yet let me not, when this morning prayer is said,
 think my worship is ended and spend the day
 in forgetfulness of you.
Rather from these moments of quietness let light go forth,
and joy, and power,
that will remain with me through all the hours of the day;
 keeping me chaste in thought;
 keeping me disciplined and truthful in speech;
 keeping me faithful and diligent in my work;
 keeping me humble in my estimation of myself;
 keeping me honourable and generous in
 my dealings with others;
 keeping me loyal to every hallowed memory of the past;
 keeping me mindful of my eternal destiny as a child of yours.

O God, who has been a refuge for many generations,
be my refuge today in every time and circumstance of need.
Be my guide through all that is dark and doubtful.
Be my guard against all that threatens my spirit's welfare.
Be my strength in time of testing.
Gladden my heart with your peace.

*John Baillie (1886-1960 )*

Loving God, who sees in humankind           *61*
nothing that you have not given yourself,
   make my body healthy and agile,
   my mind sharp and clear,
   my heart joyful and contented,
   my soul faithful and loving.
And surround me with the company of people and
   angels who share my devotion to you.
Above all, let me live in your presence,
   for with you all fear is banished
   and there is only harmony and peace.
Let every day combine the beauty of spring,
   the brightness of summer,
   the abundance of autumn
   and the repose of winter.
And at the end of my life on earth,
   grant that I may see and know you
   in the fullness of your glory.

*St. Thomas Aquinas (c. 1225-1274)*


Lord, for today,           *62*
I simply pray that I may love and be loved;
   that I may serve as you served;
   that I may give myself for my brothers and sisters.
Today, I pray that I may share your word in the
   power of the Spirit as opportunity presents itself,
   and that I may never be held back by human respect or fear.
Give me the spirit of prayer
   and of continued thanksgiving in all circumstances of life,
   especially in the difficult ones.
Heal me, Lord,
   and grant me simplicity and unity within myself,
   through Jesus Christ the Lord.

*Alan Rees OSB (b. 1941)*

63    I am only a spark:
        make me a fire.
    I am only a string:
        make me a lyre.
    I am only a drop:
        make me a fountain.
    I am only an anthill:
        make me a mountain.
    I am only a feather:
        make me a wing.
    I am only a rag:
        make me a king!

*A Mexican prayer*

64    Lord, I am growing old.
    I am slower than I used to be.
    My memory is not so good.
    The disabilities and irritations
        of old age come upon me.
    I find myself telling the same old jokes.
    Loved ones and friends pass on
        across the frontier of this life and the next.
    Lord God, I dare to ask in prayer
        if I may keep in touch with them and they with me.
    May your beloved Son,
        who brings love to us,
        take our love to them,
        for he still spans this world of creation
        and the world of full life

*George Appleton (1902-1993)*

65    Jesus, meek and humble of heart,
    make my heart like yours.

# Prayers of
# Love
# & Peace

O God, generous giver to your children,           66
    keep me from envy toward my friends and neighbours,
    and from every form of jealousy.
Teach me to rejoice in what others have which I have not,
    to delight in what they achieve which I cannot accomplish,
    to be glad in all that they enjoy which I do not share;
and so fill me daily more and more with love.

*William Angus Knight (1836-1916)*

Take all hate from my heart, O God,           67
    and teach me how to take it from the hearts of others.
Open my eyes and show me what things in our society
    make it easy for hatred to flourish
    and hard for us to conquer it.
Then help me to try to change these things.
And so open my eyes and my heart
    that I may this coming day be able
    to do some work of peace for you.

*Alan Paton (1903-1988)*

Almighty and most merciful God,           68
    you have given a new commandment
    that we should love one another.
Give me grace to fulfil it.
Make me gentle, courteous and tolerant.
Direct my life so that I may look to the good of others
    in word and deed.
Sanctify all my friendships by the blessing of your Spirit,
    for the sake of your Son Jesus Christ.

*Brooke Foss Westcott (1825-1901)*

69    Lord, help us to remember when we first met,
        and the strong love that grew between us;
        to work that love into practical things
        so nothing can divide us.
We ask for words both kind and loving,
        and hearts always ready to ask for forgiveness
        as well as to forgive.
Dear Lord, we put our marriage into your hands.

*Author unknown*

70    God of love, through your only Son
        you have given us a new commandment
        that we should love one another as you loved us,
        the unworthy and wandering.
Give to me, throughout my life on earth,
        a mind ready to forget past ill will,
        a pure conscience
        and a heart to love others.

*Coptic Liturgy of St. Cyril (5th Century)*

71    Lord God, the source of all holy desire,
good plans and right actions:
        give me your peace,
        which the world cannot give,
        so that, free from the fear of my enemies,
        I may obey your commandments
        and live in rest and quietness.
I ask this through the merits of Jesus Christ my Saviour.

*Gelasian Sacramentary (6th Century)*

O God, let us be united:
    let us speak in harmony;
    let our minds share understanding.
May we be one in our prayer,
    one in the purpose of our meeting,
    one in our resolution,
    one in all our deliberations.
Let our feelings be alike,
    our hearts be unified,
    our intentions the same.
Let our unity be perfect.

72

*Based on the Hindu Scriptures*

Lord Jesus, in you the perfect love of God is shown:
    hold me firm in this vision,
    always open to your call.
You heal all creation by the offering of your life:
    transfigure me with love,
    make me holy, make me perfect.
As you gave yourself to heal the world,
    may I give myself to you and to others.

73

*Richard Garrard (b. 1937)*

Father God,
    scripture teaches that to obey Jesus
    is to live within his love,
    just as he, in obeying you,
    lived within yours.
Help me truly to learn this,
    so that I may be filled with joy;
    let my cup of joy overflow.

74

*Based on John 15:9-11*

75   O God of many names,
lover of all nations,
I pray for peace:
   in every heart
   in every home,
   in every nation,
   throughout the world;
the peace of your will,
the peace of all our need

*George Appleton (1902-1993)*

76   At the still centre of my being,
   let me hear your voice.
   Let it carry me through to the kingdom of heaven
   that exists and breathes within me.
At the still centre of my being,
   let me hear your voice that has existed in all time,
   calling me to the union of peace and love.
At the still centre of my being,
   let the hope born with me break forth in joy.
At the still centre of my being,
   let the seeds sown in love,
   nourished in love,
   grow into bright and glorious flowers,
   rich in fruit.
At the still centre of my being,
   let me rest in love.

*Jenny Hunt*

77   Lord, make me willing to be used by you.
May my knowledge of my unworthiness
   never make me resist being used by you.
May the need of others always be remembered by me,
   so that I may ever be willing to be used by you.
And open my eyes and my heart that I may this coming day
   be able to do some work of peace for you.

*Alan Paton (1903-1988)*

O God the Father,                                                    78
    source of all that is good and true,
    in whom is calmness, peace and harmony,
    heal the dissensions which divide people from each other,
    and bring us back to a unity of love
    which may bear some likeness to your divine nature.
And as you are above all things,
    make us one by unity of thought,
    that through the bonds of love we may be one,
    both with ourselves and with each other;
    through that peace of yours which makes all things peaceful,
    and through the grace, mercy and love of your Son,
    Jesus Christ.

*St. Dionysius (6th Century)*

O Lord, enable me to greet the coming day in peace.                 79
Help me in all things to rely upon your holy will.
Throughout the day reveal your will to me.
Bless my dealings with all who surround me.
Teach me to treat all that comes to me
    throughout the day with peace of soul
    and with firm conviction that your purpose
    is at work in all things.
Guide my thoughts and feelings,
    my words and actions.
In unforeseen events,
    let me not lose sight of your presence.
Teach me to act firmly and wisely,
    without embittering and embarrassing others.
Give me strength to bear whatever stress
    the coming day may bring.
Direct my will,
    teach me to pray,
    and let your Holy Spirit pray in me.

*Metropolitan Philaret of Moscow (1782-1867)*

80    Lead me from death to life,
         from falsehood to truth.
      Lead me from despair to hope,
         from fear to trust.
      Lead me from hate to love,
         from war to peace.
      Let peace fill our heart,
         our world, our universe.

*Satish Kumar (b. 1936)*

81    May God, who brought the two of us together
         and joined us as husband and wife,
         affirm our love and make us one for ever,
         blessing us with joy each day of our life.

*Author unknown*

82    My Lord,
         I believe, and know, and feel
         that you are the supreme Good.
      I believe that all the wonder of your creation
         is of no account compared with you.
      And therefore,
         since I recognise you as being so beautiful,
         I love you and long to love you more and more.
      My God,
         you know how little I love you;
      I should not be able to love you at all,
         except for your grace.
      Keep my whole being centred on you.
      Let me never lose sight of you,
         and let my love for you grow
         more and more every day.

*John Henry Newman (1801-1890)*

My Father, may this day bring me new vision,    83
  new sense of responsibility,
  new consciousness of the joy of being
  one of your children.
Draw me into closer communion with you,
  and make me a partner in your love,
  your joy,
  your rest,
  your peace.

*J. H. Jowett (1864-1923)*


Peace, Lord, peace.    84
Help me by your peace
  to give peace,
  to radiate peace,
  to receive peace,
  to achieve peace.
Teach me by your peace
  when to forego peace,
  when to disturb peace,
  when to distil peace,
  always to be at peace,
O Lord of peace.

*David Adam*


Bless our marriage, O God,    85
  let us love one another and seek always
  to be friends rather than compete for power.
Help us to regard each other as sacred,
  and to that end,
  may we live a life of prayerful commitment,
  simplicity and self-restraint,
  through Jesus Christ our Lord.

*Based on a saying of Mahatma Gandhi (1869-1948)*

86 Father, enlarge my sympathies;
give me a roomier heart.
May my life be like a great welcoming tree
in whose shade the wanderer may rest.

Create in me the spirit of gentleness,
and let me touch the wounds of the world with gentle
compassion.
Save me from all unthinking severity
and from harshness of judgement.

*J. H. Jowett (1864-1923)*

87 Lord, keep all my children free to love.
Never let the slightest shade of suspicion shadow any heart.
Help us to think the best of each other.
Through all the chances and changes of life
hold all together in tender love.
Let nothing quench love.
Let nothing cool it.
Keep every thread of the golden cord unbroken,
unweakened, even to the end.
O my Lord, Loving One,
keep all whom I love close together
in your love for ever.

*Amy Carmichael (1867-1951)*

88 Bless our home, Father,
that we cherish the bread
before there is none,
discover each other
before we leave,
and enjoy each other
for what we are
while we have time.

*Author unknown*

Dear Lord,                                                                89
   it seems that you are so madly
   in love with your creation
   that you could not live without us.
So you created us;
   and then, when we turned away from you,
   you redeemed us.
You are God.
Your greatness is made no greater by our creation;
   your power is made no stronger by our redemption.
Yet you care for us as your own,
   not out of duty but out of love.
It is love, and love alone,
   which moves you.

*Catherine of Sienna (c.1347-1380)*

God, you gave me a child:                                                 90
   originally part of me,
   initially dependent on me,
given me to love,
   to nurture
   and to set free.
Not mine to possess
   but mine to love;
not mine to own
   but mine to respect;
not mine to grasp at
   but mine to hold.
God, give me Solomon's wisdom
   to recognise true love
   in the willingness to let go.

*Michael Forster (b. 1946)*

91   Heart of Jesus,
    burning with love for me,
inflame my heart
    with love for you.


92   My God, I love you.


93   Lord, help me to treasure stillness and rest,
for therein lies your strength.

*Based on Isaiah 30:15*


94   O God, make me a child of quietness,
an heir of peace.

*St. Clement (150-215)*


95   Jesus, for love of you, with you and for you.


96   Jesus, my God, I love you above all things.

# Prayers of Joy, Praise & Thanksgiving

I thank you, Lord, for knowing me                                    97
    better than I know myself,
and for letting me know myself
    better than others know me.
Make me, I pray,
    better than they suppose,
    and forgive me for what they do not know.

*Possibly by Abu Bekr (d. 634)*

Holy God, may the glories of your creation                           98
    awaken my heart to beauty and song.
Dispel the wintry coldness of my heart
    by the incoming of your Spirit,
    that I may know your true joy.
Refine my soul by your Spirit,
    and make me more aware of the things of true worth.
Help me to hear your still small voice.

*J. H. Jowett (1864-1923)*

O Lord my God, I pray to you, the supreme truth,                     99
    for all truth comes from you.
I bring my prayer to you the highest wisdom:
    the wise are such through you.
You are the supreme joy:
    all true happiness comes from you.
You are the highest good:
    from you all love and beauty spring.
You are the Light of the intellect:
    from you comes all human understanding.

*Adapted from King Alfred (849-899)*

100 Thanks be to you, my Lord Jesus Christ,
  for all the blessings you have won for me,
  for all the pains and insults you have borne for me.
O most merciful Redeemer, friend and brother,
  may I know you more clearly,
  love you more dearly,
  follow you more nearly,
  now and for ever.

*St. Richard of Chichester (1197-1253)*

101 Lord of all mercy and goodness,
  let me not by any ingratitude
  or hardness of heart
  forget the wonderful benefits
  that you have bestowed upon me
  this and every day;
but grant that I may be mindful,
  all the days of my life,
  of the incomparable gifts
  which you always give to me.

*Traditional Scottish prayer*

102 Glory to you, O God, creator and Father,
  for the universe in which we live,
  and for humanity, made in your own image.
Glory to you, O Christ,
  who took a human body
  and redeemed our fallen nature.
Glory to you, O Holy Spirit,
  whose will it is that we should be made whole
  in body, mind and spirit.
Glory to God to all eternity.

*George Appleton (1902-1993)*

Almighty God, Lord of heaven and earth,         *103*
in whom all creation lives and moves
and has its being:
    you are good to all people,
    making your sun to rise on the evil and on the good,
    and sending rain on the just and the unjust.
Look favourably on me your servant
as I call upon your name,
and send me your blessings from heaven,
    in giving fruitful seasons
    and meeting my needs with food and gladness;
that both my heart and my mouth
may be continually filled with your praise,
and I may ever give thanks to you in your holy church.

*John Cosin (1595-1672)*

You, Lord, have given so much to me;        *104*
    give me one thing more,
    a grateful heart.

*George Herbert (1593-1633)*

I thank you, Lord,        *105*
    that you have kept me through this day.
I thank you, Lord,
    that you will keep me through the night.
Bring me in safety, Lord,
    to the morning hours,
    that you may receive my praise at all times,
    through Jesus Christ my Lord.

*Gelasian Sacramentary (6th Century)*

106    Eternal and ever-blessed God,
     I give you thanks, as the day comes to an end,
       for those who mean so much to me
       and without whom life could never be the same.

     I thank you for those to whom I can go at any time
       and never feel a nuisance.

     I thank you for those to whom I can go when I am tired,
       knowing that they have,
       for weary feet,
       the gift of rest.

     I thank you for those with whom I can talk,
       and keep nothing back,
       knowing that they will not laugh at my dreams
       or mock my failures.

     I thank you for those in whose presence
       it is easier to be good.

     I thank you for those in whose company joys are increased
       and sorrow's bitterness is soothed.

     I thank you for those who by their timely warning and
       their criticism
       have helped me avoid mistakes I might have made
       and sins I might have committed.

And above all,
I thank you for Jesus,
     the pattern for my life,
     the Lord of my heart
     and the Saviour of my soul.

Accept this my thanksgiving,
     and grant me tonight a good night's rest;
     through Jesus Christ my Lord.

*William Barclay (1907-1978)*

Praise be to you, O God,                                                    107
    who answer me when I call upon you,
    slow though I am to answer you when you call me.
Praise be to you, O God,
    who give to me when I ask,
    miserly though I am when you ask of me.
Praise be to you, O God,
    to whom I confide my needs and they are satisfied.
Praise be to you, O God,
    for you are most worthy of praise.

*Based on a Muslim prayer*


Arising from sleep,                                                         108
I fall down before you,
O blessed God,
and join in the angelic hymn:
    Holy, holy, holy are you, O God.
    Have mercy upon me, I pray.

*Eastern Orthodox*


Set my heart on fire with love for you, O Christ my God,                    109
that in its flame I may love you with all my heart,
    with my mind,
    with all my soul
    and with all my strength,
    and my neighbour as myself,
so that keeping your commandments I may glorify you,
the giver of all good gifts.

*Kontakion (Eastern Orthodox)*

110    I adore you, O Christ, and I praise you,
        because by your holy cross
        you have redeemed the world.

*Traditional*

111    O God, I thank you for this universe;
        for its vastness and its riches,
        and for the variety of life which teems within it
        and of which I am a part.
    I praise you for the sky and the winds,
        for the clouds
        and for the constellations of the heavens.
    I praise you for seas and rivers,
        for mountains and trees,
        and the grass beneath my feet.
    I thank you for the senses which enable
        me to see the splendour of the morning,
        to hear the songs of the birds,
        and enjoy the scents of springtime.
    Open my heart, I pray,
        to all this joy and beauty,
        and save me from being so burdened by care
        or blinded by greed
        that I fail to notice when even the thornbushes
        are aflame with your glory.

*Walter Rauschenbusch (1861-1918)*

112    To you be praise,
    to you be glory,
    to you be thanksgiving,
        through endless ages,
        O blessed Trinity.

*Author unknown*

I thank you, God, for the saints of all ages,           *113*
for those who in times of darkness
   kept the lamp of faith burning,
for the great souls who saw visions of larger truths
   and dared to declare them,
for the multitude of quiet, gracious souls
   whose presence purified and sanctified the world;
and for those known and loved by us who have passed
   from this earthly fellowship into the fuller life with you.
Accept this our thanksgiving, through Jesus Christ,
   to whom be praise and dominion for ever.

*Fellowship Litanies*

O Lord, I praise and glorify you           *114*
for all the benefits I have received;
I bless you, I thank you,
my heart sings of your great goodness,
and in humble love I acclaim you.
Glory be to you, my benefactor and saviour.

*Eastern Orthodox*

O God, I know you love me!           *115*
My heart is all joy because of what you have done for me.
How good you have been to me, O God most high;
   in my joy I shall sing and delight.
I shall sing in your honour.

*Carmelite Monastery, Quidenham*

116 Let all homage be given to you, Perfect Wisdom:
    you are boundless, you are above all human thought;
    you are faultless, you are without blemish;
    you are spotless, you are greater than space itself.

As the moonlight depends on the moon,
    so all wisdom depends on your wisdom.
As the sunlight depends on the sun,
    so all virtue depends on your virtue.

Those who are constantly concerned with the welfare of others
    are blessed by you in their efforts.
You are like a mother to the soul,
    giving birth to love, and nourishing virtue.

As the stars dance round the moon,
    so righteous souls dance round your throne.
As white clouds encircle the sun,
    so pure souls encircle your throne.

As the drops of dew evaporate
    when the hot rays of the sun appear,
    so all evil and falsehood evaporate
    under the warmth of your love and truth.

There are some who have no affection for you,
    and some who look upon you with hatred.
You do not condemn or destroy them,
    but they condemn themselves to hopeless misery.

Never to look upon your brightness,
    never to hear your eternal music,
    never to feel your softness,
    is to live without pleasure or joy.

Those who are devoted to you
    are slaves to your power.
Yet in obeying your commands of love,
    the soul finds perfect freedom.

Those who are cold and indifferent to you
  imagine they enjoy perfect freedom.
Yet they are slaves to their own desires,
  bound in chains by their bodily warmth.

You are the only path to salvation;
  there is no other way but you.
You are the saviour of the world;
  the world is lost without you.

No words can properly describe you;
  the soul alone can know you.
The silent love of the soul
  is the true chorus of praise.

*Rahulabhdra (2nd Century)*


Jesus, when I am with you I burn with joy.                    *117*
And when the heat of love surges within me,
  I want to embrace you, to clasp you to myself.
Yet, my love is frustrated by a strange,
  invisible barrier that seems
  to stand between me and you.
If only you would break down that barrier,
  and so let me rush into your arms.
I can see you clearly,
  and I beg you to allow me to come to you.
I am in prison, beating my fists against the wall
  that divides me from you.
But in the meantime I can sing your praises,
  and in prayer I can speak with you.
So I will enjoy such blessings for the present,
  in the hope of being united fully in the future.

*Richard Rolle (c. 1300-1349)*

118 May you be blessed for ever, Lord,
    for not abandoning me when I abandoned you.
May you be blessed for ever, Lord,
    for offering your hand of love in my darkest,
    most lonely moments.
May you be blessed for ever, Lord,
    for putting up with such a stubborn soul as mine.
May you be blessed for ever, Lord,
    for loving me more than I love myself.
May you be blessed for ever, Lord,
    for continuing to pour out your blessings upon me,
    even though I respond so poorly.
May you be blessed for ever, Lord,
    for drawing out the goodness in all people,
    even including me.
May you be blessed for ever, Lord,
    for repaying my sin with your love.
May you be blessed for ever, Lord,
    for being constant and unchanging
    amidst all the changes of the world.
May you be blessed for ever, Lord,
    for your countless blessings on me
    and on all your creatures.

*St. Teresa of Avila (1515-1582)*

119 Praised be Jesus Christ,
    now and for ever.

120 Blessing and glory
    and wisdom and thanksgiving,
    honour, might and power
    be ascribed to God for ever and ever.

# Prayers of
# Trust
# & Hope

My Lord God,  *121*
I have no idea where I am going.
I do not see the road ahead of me.
I cannot know for certain where it will end.
Nor do I really know my own self,
    and the fact that I think I am following your will
    does not mean that I am actually doing so.
But I believe that the desire to please you
    does in fact please you.
And I hope I have that desire in all that I am doing.
I hope that I will never do anything
    except with that desire.
And I do know that if I do this,
    you will lead me by the right road
    though I may know nothing about it.
Therefore I will trust you always
    though I may seem lost and in the shadow of death.
I will not fear, for you are ever with me,
    and you will never leave me to face my perils alone.

*Thomas Merton (1915-1968)*

O Lord, when I awake and day begins,  *122*
    waken me to your presence;
    waken me to your indwelling Spirit;
    waken me to inward sight of you,
    and speech with you,
    and strength from you;
that all my earthly walk may waken into song
    and my spirit leap up to you all day,
    all ways.

*Eric Milner-White (1884-1964)*

123   Into your hands, heavenly Father,
         I place this new day.
      You know how wayward I am;
         you know how quickly my thoughts stray from you
         and from Jesus, the way, the truth and the life.
      I ask you to give me your Holy Spirit
         in good measure this day;
         may he be my guide.
      May he govern every detail of my life,
         however small and insignificant.
      May he fill me with love and praise,
         so that every moment of this day may belong to you.
      Without you, O holy and blessed Trinity,
         my life lacks purpose,
         but filled with the gift of the Holy Spirit
         it takes on the dimension of your glory.
      Stay with me, great God,
         and enable me to live for the praise of your glory.
      I ask this in Jesus' name.

*Alan Rees OSB (b. 1941)*


124   Help me to remember, Lord God,
         that every day is your gift
         and ought to be used according to your will.

*Samuel Johnson (1709-1784)*


125   Lighten my darkness, Lord, I pray,
         and in your great mercy defend me from
         all perils and dangers of this night,
         for the sake of your only Son,
         my Saviour Jesus Christ.

*Gelasian Sacramentary (6th Century)*

Help me, Lord, to let go of whatever keeps my life       *126*
    from being the best it can be:
    the stress, the frustration, the anger,
    the petty jealousies and strong temptations.
Help me to let go of the need to feel
    that I am in sole charge of my life.
Help me to trust you for the strength I need,
    and guide me to that still,
    serene place within myself.
Help me to trust you to show me your way,
    and give me courage and wisdom to follow it.
May I find renewed peace by committing my life to you.

*Author unknown*

Be present, O merciful God,       *127*
    and protect me through the silent hours of this night,
    so that I who am wearied by the changes
    and chances of this fleeting world
    may rest upon your eternal changelessness;
    through Jesus Christ my Lord.

*The Office of Compline*

Lord, you are always with me.       *128*
No weakness can keep you away,
    no besetting sin.
In all seasons,
    at all times,
    you are with me,
    until we meet again
    in your kingdom.

*Graham Jeffery (b. 1935)*

129    What shall I say in your presence,
        you who dwell on high?
    What shall I declare to you,
        who are in heaven beyond?
    For you know things secret
        as well as revealed.
    You know the mysteries of the universe
        and the unconscious thoughts of everyone alive.
    You search the innermost parts,
        you watch my motives and my passions.
    Nothing is concealed from you.
    Nothing is hidden from your gaze.

    Lord my God, and God of my ancestors,
        have mercy upon me and pardon my sins.
    Forgive my wrongdoing and set aside my misdeeds.
    Blot out the wrong that I have done,
        for you, O Lord, are good and forgiving,
        and full of love to all who call upon you.
    For your own sake, forgive my great failure.
    For your own sake, give me life.
    In your righteousness bring my soul out of trouble.
    The Lord of all creation is with me.
    The God of Jacob is my refuge.
    Lord of creation,
        happy are those who trust in you.

*Reform Synagogues of Great Britain*

130    Save me, O Lord, while I am awake,
        and guard me while I sleep,
        that awake I may watch with Christ,
        and asleep I may rest in peace,
        in Jesus' name.

*The Office of Compline*

Lord, whose way is perfect,                                              *131*
help me always to trust in your goodness,
that walking with you
and following you in all simplicity,
I may possess a quiet and contented mind
and may cast all care on you,
for you care for me.

*Christina Rosetti (1830-1894)*


Lord Jesus Christ, Saviour and Redeemer,                                 *132*
I ask you to be Lord of my sleep;
   be Lord of my resting and of my rising;
   be Lord of my dreams.
Do not let the evil one approach me in the hours of my sleep.
Breathe the gentle breath of the Holy Spirit
   into my heart during these hours of unconsciousness;
   even while I sleep let him be my teacher and guide.
Speak your word to my heart
   – words of peace and consolation.
Lift me up into the Father's arms,
   way above the cares and anxieties,
   the temptations and sufferings of this life;
   way above the snares and deceits of the devil.
Let me rest surrounded by the Father's love,
   secure in the salvation won for me
   by your precious blood,
   and abiding in the resurrection joy
   through the power of the Holy Spirit.
I make this prayer in your name, Jesus,
   for to you, together with the eternal Father
   and the life giving Spirit,
   belong all power, glory,
   might, majesty and praise.
Amen. Alleluia.

*Alan Rees OSB (b. 1941)*

133   Holy God, you have shown me light and life.
      You are stronger than any natural power.
      Accept the words from my heart
          that struggle to reach you.
      Accept the silent thoughts and feelings
          that are offered to you.
      Clear my mind of the clutter of useless facts.
      Bend down to me, and lift me up in your arms.
      Make me holy as you are holy.
      Give me a voice to sing of your love to others.

                    *From a papyrus (probably 2nd-4th century)*


134   Father, make me realise more and more
          that it is only in being stripped of everything
          that I am more given to you;
          and when I am more given to you,
          then am I truly free.
      Let me cling to nothing;
          let me lose all to gain all.
      Let me never rely on myself;
          when I cannot cope
          let me hand everything over to you
          and just trust you,
          remembering that I am your child
          and you care for me.
      Let me accept humiliation and the cross with Jesus crucified.
      Let me remain hidden and humble in union with your Son.
      Let me always remember
          that the only thing that matters
          is to be totally united with your will
          and in this is my peace.
      Let my prayer be always Amen! Alleluia!

                    *Alan Rees OSB (b. 1941)*

Lord, when I think only of my own wants and desires,      *135*
I am impatient to have them satisfied;
    yet in my heart I know that such satisfaction
    will crumble to dust.
Give me that spirit of hope which can
    enable me to want what you want,
    and to wait patiently on your time
    in the knowledge that in you alone
    is found true and lasting pleasure.

*Mozarabic Sacramentary (3rd century)*

O Christ Jesus,      *136*
    my helper and my redeemer.

My soul truly waits on you, O God,      *137*
    since my salvation comes from you.

*Psalm 62:1*

My God and my all.      *138*

Lord, may I be still in your presence,      *139*
    and wait patiently for you.

*Psalm 37*

Give me grace, Lord, to be still      *140*
    and know that you are God.

*Psalm 46:10*

# Prayers of
# Repentance
# &
# Forgiveness

Deliver, O most merciful God,      141
 all who have strayed into evil ways.
Do not remember their wrongdoing
 but set them free from enslavement to evil.
Bless by the power of your Holy Spirit the efforts of all
 who are seeking to influence them for good;
 and grant that, sharing in your heavenly wisdom,
 they may be strengthened to follow your ways.

       *Robert Leighton (1611-1684)*


Most merciful Father,        142
I confess that I have done little
 to promote your kingdom
 and advance your glory.
Pardon my shortcomings
 and give me greater enthusiasm in serving you.
Make me more ready
 and conscientious by my prayers,
 my giving and my example,
 to spread the knowledge of your truth
 and extend your kingdom;
 and may I do everything to your glory.

     *William Walsham How (1823-1897)*


Lord Jesus, heal me of the wounds of yesterday  143
 that I may live abundantly today
and with confidence in your Providence
 go forward into tomorrow.

       *Alan Rees OSB (b. 1941)*

144   Lord God almighty,
      forgive your church
         its wealth among the poor,
         its fear among the unjust,
         its cowardice among the oppressed;
      forgive us, your children,
         our lack of confidence in you,
         our lack of hope in your reign,
         our lack of faith in your presence,
         our lack of trust in your mercy.
      Restore us to your covenant with your people;
         bring us to true repentance;
         teach us to accept the sacrifice of Christ;
         make us strong with the comfort of your Holy Spirit.
      Break us where we are proud;
         make us where we are weak;
         shame us where we trust ourselves;
         name us where we have lost ourselves.

*World Council of Churches*


*Did I not tell you that if you believe in me*
*you will see the glory of God? (John 11:40)*

145   Lord, take away the stone from the entrance to my heart.
      Let out the stench of corruption, decay and death
         that has been there so long;
      let the new person emerge,
         no longer bound by past sins
         but unbound and made free by your healing love.

'Take off the grave clothes and let him go!'

*Alan Rees OSB (b. 1941)*

O Lord my God,        146
    forgive me the sins I have committed this day
    in thought, word or deed,
    for you are gracious and you love all people.
Grant me peaceful, undisturbed sleep;
    send your guardian angel
    to protect and guard me from every evil,
    for you are the guardian of my soul and body,
    and to you is ascribed glory,
    Father, Son and Holy Spirit,
    now and for ever.

*Russian Orthodox*


I love you, Lord Jesus, above all things;     147
I repent with my whole heart of ever having offended you.
Give me grace not to separate myself from you again.
Grant that I may love you always,
    and then let me serve you as you will.

*St. Alphonsus Liguori (1696-1787)*


O Lord, remember not only the men and women of good will,   148
    but also those of evil will.
But do not remember all the suffering
    they have inflicted upon us;
remember the fruits we have bought, thanks to this suffering:
    our comradeship, our loyalty, our humility,
    our courage, our generosity,
    the greatness of heart which has grown out of all this;
and when they come to judgment,
    let all the fruits we have borne
    be their forgiveness.

*Found near a child's body in Ravensbruch*
*Women's Concentration Camp*

149   Make me simple and humble, O Lord.
Give me the full blessing of your Spirit,
    not for my own consolation and delight
    but for your glory,
    for your church.
Last time, I went wrong,
I was too quick, too eager.
I looked for an escape from what was around
    because I was afraid.
The Holy Spirit is not an escape
    but an immersion in reality, in Christ.
How could I have been so slow-witted
    and dull not to realise the effect?
I was selfish then and I have realised it,
    but that was a beginning,
    even though there has been a lapse, a serious lapse,
    when I forgot you because there were other things;
    and although they hurt so much, so very much,
    yet I preferred them to you
    because they were easier,
    more accessible, or seemed to be.
God, make me humble,
    simple, open,
    and let the Spirit transform me
    as he transformed the Twelve and Mary in Jerusalem.
Let him transform me,
    not for my comfort or tranquillity
    but for your glory
    and the building up of your kingdom.
Slake my thirst for you,
God, living God,
living Water, Rock, Manna,
Life, Light, Love!

*Alan Rees OSB (b. 1941)*

150   Lord Jesus Christ, son of God,
    have mercy on me, a sinner.

*The Jesus Prayer*

Lord Christ, who prayed for those who crucified you     *151*
and commanded your disciples to pray for their enemies,
   forgive those who hate and maltreat me,
   and turn my life from all harm and evil
   to love shown in action.
For this I humbly pray,
   that, united with all creation,
   I may glorify you
   who alone has perfect love for all people.

*Eastern Orthodox*


Forgive my sins, O Lord;     *152*
   the sins of my present and the sins of my past,
   the sins which I have done to please myself,
   and the sins which I have done to please others.
Forgive my casual sins and my deliberate sins,
   and those which I have tried so hard to hide
   that I have hidden them even from myself.
Forgive me, O Lord, for all of them,
   for Jesus Christ's sake.

*Thomas Wilson (1663-1755)*


O Holy Spirit of God,     *153*
   cleanse my eyes to see as you see;
   cleanse my ears to hear you speaking to me;
   cleanse my lips to speak only your words;
   cleanse my mind to discern clearly what is from you;
   cleanse my heart and fill it with your love,
   love that will overflow to all your people;
   cleanse my body and make it more and more your temple;
to the glory and praise of the Father.

*Alan Rees OSB (b. 1941)*

154   Crucified Jesus,
      I kneel in your presence and contemplate in my mind
          the five wounds of your crucifixion.
      I earnestly pray to be filled
         with the gifts of faith, hope and love,
         with true repentance for my sinfulness
         and a firm intention to change.
      So may the contemplation of your passion be for me
         the means of atonement and salvation.

*Based on a traditional prayer*

155   O God, we bring you our failure,
         our hunger, our disappointment, our despair,
         our greed, our aloofness, our loneliness.
      When we cling to others in desperation,
         or turn from them in fear,
         strengthen us in love.
      Teach us, women and men,
         to use our power with care.
      We turn to you O God,
         we renounce evil,
         we claim your love,
         we choose to be made whole.

*The St. Hilda Community*

156   My Father, on this new day
         may I experience your great renewal.
      May my duties, my sympathies,
         my aspirations be renewed.
      May I experience a new heaven
         and a new earth.

*J. H. Jowett (1864-1923)*

O God my Father,         *157*
   you know how often I fail because I am afraid.
I fear what people will do if I stand for the right;
I fear what they will say.
I fear that I shall not have the strength to go on,
   even if I begin.
Forgive me for my weakness.
Help me to remember Christ
   and all that he endured for me,
      so that I, like him, may never be afraid of people
      but only of sinning against your love.
I ask it for his name's sake.

*A. G. Pite*

Heavenly Father, I confess my sins to you:     *158*
   the sins of the past and of the present;
   those hidden and forgotten
   as well as those remembered;
   my sins of thought and desire,
   of word, of deed and of omission;
   the sins that I am too dull of heart to see;
   the sins that others can see and I cannot;
   the sins known to you alone.
I am sorry for all of them.

I ask you to forgive me
   through the merit of Jesus, my Saviour.
Please renew your life in me
   by the power of the Holy Spirit.

*Alan Rees OSB (b. 1941)*

O Lord, grant this day         *159*
   to keep me without sin.

160  O God, forgive me for all the faults
    which make me difficult to live with.

    If I behave as if I were the only person for whom
        life is difficult;
      if I behave as if I were far harder worked than anyone else;
      if I behave as if I were the only person ever to be
        disappointed or to get a raw deal;
      if I am far too self-centred and far too full of self-pity:
    forgive me, O God.

    If I am too impatient to finish the work I have begun;
      if I am too impatient to listen to someone
        who wants to talk to me,
      or to give someone a helping hand;
      if I think that other people are fools,
        and make no attempt to conceal my contempt for them:
    forgive me, O God.

    If I too often rub people up the wrong way;
      if I spoil a good case by trying to ram it
        down someone's throat;
      if I do things that get on people's nerves,
        and go on doing them even when I am asked not to:
    forgive me, O God.

    Help me to take the selfishness and the ugliness out of life
      and to do better in the days to come.

*William Barclay (1907-1978)*


161  O Lord and master of my life,
    take from me the spirit of laziness, faint-heartedness,
    lust for power, and love of gossip.
  Give me grace to see my own errors and not to judge others,
    for you are blessed from all ages to all ages.

*Eastern Orthodox*

Lord, in your loving kindness,        162
   give me the fullness of the Holy Spirit
   to establish me in abundant life.
Grant that I may be a better person,
   more loving, more attentive
   and more generous to you and to everyone.

Grant me the Spirit of new life and of healing,
   so that I may be whole in body and soul.
Let your Spirit destroy in me
   the roots of sin and fear;
may he take from me all hardness of heart
   and plant within me your law of love
so that I may grow up into graciousness of life
   and find joy therein.

*Alan Rees OSB (b. 1941)*

O Light everlasting, surpassing all created light!    163
Pour forth from heaven the glorious rays of your light,
   and pierce the dark depths of my soul.
Purify, gladden and enlighten my soul,
   that it may turn to you in joy.
I know that the shadow of sin still hangs over me;
I know that I fight against your light,
   preferring the gloom of worldly pride
   to the bright sunshine of true humility.
Yet you, who can make the raging sea calm,
   can bring peace to my soul.
You, who turn night into day,
   can bring gladness to my miserable soul.
Act now!
Banish darkness at this very moment!
Inspire my soul with your love at the next breath I take!

*Thomas à Kempis (c.1380-1471)*

164    Lord, forgive me my sins:
        my lack of faith,
        my lack of hope,
        my lack of love.
    I look to you,
        kind and gracious God.
    My heart is open.
    Please give me
    Faith, Hope and Love.

*Alan Rees OSB (b. 1941)*

165    Lord, when I think that my heart is overflowing with love
        and realise in a moment's honesty that it is only
        myself that I love in the loved one,
        deliver me from myself.

    Lord, when I think I have given all that I have to give
        and realise in a moment's honesty that
        it is I who am the recipient,
        deliver me from myself.

    Lord, when I have convinced myself that I am poor
        and realise in a moment's honesty that
        I am rich in pride and envy,
        deliver me from myself.

    And, Lord, when the kingdom of heaven merges deceptively
        with the kingdoms of this world,
        let nothing satisfy me but you.

*Mother Teresa (b. 1910)*

166    Remember, Lord, what you have promised,
        giving your servant great hope.
    However low I fall,
        to that promise I cling,
    for with you, my God, lies forgiveness.

*Carmelite Monastery, Quidenham*

# Prayers of
# Faith &
# Commitment

My God, you have created me
    to do you some definite service;
you have given some definite work to me
    which you have not given to any other.
I have my place in your plan.
I may never know what it is in this life
    but I shall be told it in the next.
Therefore I will trust you in all things.
If I am sick, my sickness may serve you.
If I am worried, my worry may serve you.
If I am in sorrow, my sorrow may serve you.
Nothing is in vain:
    all things may serve your purpose.
I may lose my friends and find myself among strangers;
I may feel forgotten so that my spirits sink;
my future may be hidden from me;
still, you work in all things for good,
    and I trust you.

*John Henry Newman (1801-1890)*

O Lord, this is my desire:
to walk along the path of life
that you have appointed for me,
    in steadfastness of faith,
    in lowliness of heart,
    in gentleness of love.
Let not the cares or duties of this life
    press upon me too heavily,
    but lighten my burden
    that I may follow your way in quietness,
    filled with thankfulness for your mercy.

*Maria Hare (1798-1870)*

169  O God, I humbly pray that you will
　　　　purify my heart from all vain,
　　　　worldly and sinful thoughts,
　　　　and so prepare my soul to worship you well today
　　　　with reverence and holy awe.
　　　Focus my attention on things above, all the day long,
　　　　and give me grace to receive your word
　　　　into an honest and open heart,
　　　　and bear fruit with patience.

*Gavin Hamilton (1561-1612)*

170  Thank you, Lord, for this new day.
　　　Thank you for the people you will put in my way:
　　　　people wounded by life,
　　　　by sin, by others;
　　　　broken people created by you for love
　　　　but not experiencing it.

　　　Thank you for them.
　　　Let me never add to their burden, to their grief.

　　　Use me for them,
　　　　if only in a smile and an encouraging word
　　　　to bring them life and light.

　　　Let me live in the truth today, Lord;
　　　　let your truth become my truth
　　　　and please set me free in the process.
　　　Let me abide in you and let your word,
　　　　your will become my home.

*Alan Rees OSB (b. 1941)*

O Lord, give me more love,                                          *171*
    more self-denial,
    more likeness to you.
Teach me to sacrifice my comforts to others,
    to set aside my own preferences
    for the sake of doing good.
Make me kind in thought,
    gentle in word,
    generous in deed.
Teach me that it is better to give than to receive,
    better to forget myself than to put myself forward,
    better to serve than to be served.
And to you, the God of love,
    be all glory and praise,
    now and for ever.

*Henry Alford (1810-1871)*

Teach me, good Lord,                                               *172*
not to complain about excessive work
    or shortness of time;
not to exaggerate the tasks I undertake
    by pretending to be burdened by them;
    but to accept them all in freedom and joy.
Teach me not to call attention to busyness
    or petty irritations;
not to become so dependent upon others' appreciation of me
    that my motives become suspect;
not to demand respect from other people
    merely on account of my age or past achievements.

*Edward Benson (1829-1896)*

173   I ask you, O God, the God of truth,
      that what I ought to know you will teach me,
      that where I am mistaken you will correct me,
      that whenever I stumble you will support me,
        and from all that is false,
        all that is damaging,
        you will always protect me.

*Brooke Foss Westcott (1825-1901)*


174   O heavenly Father, in whom I live and move
        and have my being,
      I humbly pray that you will guide me by your Holy Spirit
        that in all the cares and occupations of my daily life
        I may never forget you,
        but remember that I am always walking in your sight.

*Author Unknown*


175   O Lord, to whom everything in heaven and earth belongs,
      I long to commit myself wholly to you
        and be yours for ever.
      I offer myself to you wholeheartedly today
        to serve and obey you
        and offer you constant sacrifice
        of praise and thanksgiving.
      Accept me, my Saviour,
        with the offering of your body and blood,
        in the presence of the angels,
        that this sacrifice may be sufficient
        for the redemption of myself
        and the whole creation.

*Thomas à Kempis (1380-1471)*

Help me at all times, O God,                                    *176*
    to encourage and not to dishearten,
    to be more ready to praise than to condemn,
    to uplift rather than to disparage,
    to veil rather than to expose the faults of others.

O risen and exalted Christ, dwell in me,
    that I may live with the light of hope in my eyes,
    the word of life on my lips
    and your love in my heart.

Help me, O Holy spirit,
    to seek you faithfully,
    to hold to you firmly,
    to show you unfailingly,
    for Christ's sake.

    *T. Glyn Thomas (1905-1973) Tr. W. Rhys Nicholas (b. 1914)*

Take, Lord, all my liberty.                                    *177*
Receive my memory,
    my understanding
    and my whole will.
Whatever I have and possess you have given me;
    to you I restore it wholly
    and to your will I utterly surrender it
    for you to direct me.
Give me love for you only,
    with your grace,
    and I am rich enough;
    nor do I ask for anything else.

    *St. Ignatius Loyola (1491-1556)*

178    All I ask, Lord, is that
      your glory may shine forth in this place.

    All I ask is that
      you give us what is best for us all and for each one.

    All I ask is that
      we may love you and each other personally
      and with our whole heart.

    Help me to surrender all my vain wishes,
      anxieties and desires
      and give all things into your waiting hands.
    Grant me the faith and trust
      that accepts everything from you as a grace,
      a blessing and an opportunity for growth.
    If this causes pain, let me accept it
      and understand it as a transforming experience.
    Help me not to put obstacles in the way of your will,
      nor to give in to sadness and anxiety
      when there is darkness and conflict in my life.

*Alan Rees OSB (b. 1941)*


179    Lord, make me so sensitive
      to the needs of those around me
      that I never fail to know
      when they are hurting or afraid;
    or when they are simply crying out
      for someone's touch
      to ease their loneliness.
    Let me love so much
      that my first thought is of others
      and my last thought is of me.

*Author unknown*

Give me courage, O Lord, to stand up and be counted, 180
   to stand up for those who cannot stand up for themselves,
   to stand up for myself when it is appropriate for me to do so.
Let me fear nothing more than I fear failing you.
Let me love nothing more than I love you,
   for thus I shall fear nothing indeed.
Let me have no other God before you,
   whether nation, or party, or state, or church.
Let me seek no other peace
   but the peace which is yours,
   and make myself its instrument,
   opening my mind and my heart
   so that I shall always know
   what work of peace I may do for you.

*Alan Paton (1903-1988)*

Lord, make me an instrument of your peace: 181
   where there is hatred, let me sow love,
   where there is injury, pardon,
   where there is doubt, faith,
   where there is darkness, light,
   where there is despair, hope,
   and where there is sadness, joy.

Divine Master,
grant that I may not so much seek
   to be consoled as to console,
   to be understood as to understand,
   to be loved as to love.
For it is in giving that we receive,
   it is in pardoning that we are pardoned,
   and in dying that we are born to eternal life.

*Attributed to St. Francis of Assisi (1181-1226)*

182    Lord Jesus,
        I give you my hands to do your work.
        I give you my feet to go your way.
        I give you my eyes to see as you do.
        I give you my tongue to speak your words.
        I give you my mind that you may think in me.
        I give you my spirit that you may pray in me.
    Above all
        I give you my heart that you may love in me
        your Father and all humankind.
        I give you my whole self that you may grow in me,
        so that it is you, Lord Jesus,
        who live and work and pray in me.

*The Grail Prayer*


183    Teach me, good Lord,
        to serve you as you deserve:
        to give, and not to count the cost;
        to fight, and not to heed the wounds;
        to toil, and not to seek for rest;
        to labour, and to ask for no reward,
        except that of knowing that I do your will;
        through Jesus Christ my Lord.

*St. Ignatius Loyola (1491-1556)*


184    Guide me, O Lord,
        in all the changes and uncertainties of the world,
        that I remain at peace.
    Let me not complain in trouble,
        nor grow proud in prosperity,
        but in calm faith accept your will,
        through Jesus Christ my Lord.

*Jeremy Taylor (1613-1667)*

Lord, make your will my will in all things.                    185

*Charles John Vaughan (1816-1897)*


Lord, make my heart a haven                                    186
   where the lonely may find friendship,
   where the weary may find shelter,
   where the helpless may find refuge,
   where the hopeless may find hope,
   where all those who seek someone who cares
   may enter and find you.

*Author unknown*


Help me, O God, to serve you and your world well today.        187
May I do my work carefully,
   help others without indulging in ostentation,
   enjoy your gifts of food and drink,
   but without vulgarity or excess,
   and be a good friend to others.
Then may I go to bed contented and sleep well,
through Jesus Christ my Lord.

*Based on a Medieval prayer*


From the cowardice that dare not face new truth,               188
   from the laziness that is content with half truth,
   from the arrogance that thinks it knows all truth,
Good Lord, deliver me.

*Kenyan prayer*

189    Thank you, Father, for your faithful love
that has called me and borne with me
all through this journey.
I'm constantly astonished that you don't give up on me,
and yet I know you won't.
It isn't just that you put up with me, Lord,
as I disappoint you time after time;
it's much more positive than that.
    You make me understand that in some way
    the failures can be worked into your plan.
    You can contain failures.
    You use them for our growth,
    like good manure.
    You are not going to be baulked in your love.

When I think I am standing before you, trying to pray,
I often know that the reality is something other.
It's not a matter of me trying to serve you,
to love others for your sake,
to work for them and for you and to pray to you.
    No, somehow that's not right,
    because you are much closer than that.
    At the spring of my longing, you are longing;
    in the stretch of my understanding, you are there in your truth.
    In my joy, you dance in your threefold delight.
The rest is silence.

*Maria Boulding OSB*

190    Here I am, Lord – body, heart and soul.
Grant that, with your love,
I may be big enough to reach the world,
and small enough to be at one with you.

*Mother Teresa (b. 1910)*

Lord, I know you created me                                              *191*
    for a special purpose,
    to serve you in a unique way.
You have given me a gift, and talents,
    a certain something no-one else has.
Help me to be a valuable link
    in the chain of humanity.
Help me to find peace and meaning
    in what I do,
    knowing that no-one else can be me.

*Author unknown*

Lord Jesus, lead me, give me the spirit of prayer.            *192*
Teach me to pray, as you taught your apostles;
    give me courage to go with you
    into the lonely mountains
    and pray to the Father in the secret of my heart.
Teach me to struggle in prayer
    as you struggled in the garden of Gethsemane.
Draw me closer to yourself and to the Father
    through the Holy Spirit.
Help me to overcome all obstacles,
    and teach me not to be afraid
    when I have to face certain things within myself
    which seem to be more than I can cope with.
Help me in naked faith to go on knowing that you are there,
    calling me and drawing me,
    even when all seems dark and arid.
Give me the strength of the Spirit to overcome my fear.
Deepen my friendship with you;
    although I am not worthy of such a gift,
    I know that you want me to have it,
    so I take heart and come to you confidently,
    trusting in the promises you have made.

*Alan Rees OSB (b. 1941)*

193 Lord Christ,
  you have no body on earth but ours,
  no hands but ours,
  no feet but ours.
 Ours are the eyes through which your compassion
  must look out on the world.
 Ours are the feet by which you may still
  go about doing good.
 Ours are the hands with which
  you bless people now.
 Bless our minds and bodies,
  that we may be a blessing to others.

*Based on a prayer by St. Teresa of Avila (1515-1582)*

194 May I do all the good I can,
  by all the means I can,
  in all the ways I can,
  in all the places I can,
  for all the people I can,
  as long as ever I can,
 for Christ's sake.

*Based on the Rule of John Wesley (1703-1791)*

195 Lord, put courage into my heart,
  and take away all that may hinder my serving you.
 Free my tongue to proclaim your goodness,
  that all may understand me.
 Give me friends to advise and help me,
  that by working together
  our efforts may bear abundant fruit.
 And, above all,
 let me constantly remember that my actions are worthless
 unless they are guided by your hand.

*Muhammed (570-632)*

Holy God, give me true faith in you.                    *196*
In times of doubt and questioning,
   when my belief is confused by new learning,
   new teaching, new thought,
   when my faith is strained by creeds, by doctrines,
   by mysteries beyond my understanding,
give me the faithfulness of a disciple
and the courage of a believer in you;
give me confidence to examine,
   and faith to trust in, all truth;
stability to hold fast to what is good,
with the benefit of new insights and interpretations;
to acknowledge when fresh truth has been revealed to me,
and in troublesome times genuinely to grasp new knowledge
and to combine it loyally and honestly with the old;
give me the insight to refrain
both from stubborn rejection of new revelations
and from the easy assumption that mine is a more
   enlightened generation.
Save me and help me,
I humbly pray, O Lord.

*George Ridding (1828-1904)*


Lord, make me a messenger                    *197*
   of your love.
To the searching heart
   send me with your word;
to the aching heart
   send me with your peace;
to the broken heart
   send me with your love.
However small or wide
   my world, Lord,
let me warm it with the promise
   that you care.

*Author unknown*

198   Father, you have always been there,
       even from my earliest years,
       gently leading me on.
  Just as you were present in the time of the Exodus,
       a pillar of cloud by day and a pillar of fire by night,
       leading the Hebrew people out of bondage into freedom,
       so it is with me.
  You have always been there, Lord,
       leading me out of darkness into your wonderful light;
       from ignorance into truth;
       from the isolation of self into the community of love.

  Despite my wanderings,
       despite my complaining,
       despite my unwillingness to go forward,
       you have never deserted me.
  You have always remained faithful in the midst of my infidelity.

  In the daytime of my joy,
       your hidden brightness,
       the wisdom of the Holy Spirit,
       has gone before me and drawn me after it;
  in the night-time of my isolation, despondency and fear,
       your pillar of fire,
       the refining Spirit,
       has been there working in my heart,
       thawing my iciness and purifying me.
  Who can resist you, great God,
       ever seeking after us
       and compelling us to run to the light of your truth
       and the warmth of your love?

  But, Father, pilgrim that I am,
       I still wander into the byways of pride,
       self-pity and fear.
  I take my eyes off the goal all too often,
  I allow my weariness to lessen my response to your infinite love.
  Forgive me as I turn my eyes back to you.

Sharpen my awareness of your Son, Jesus, my brother,
   who takes me by the hand
   and pulls me along in my reluctance.
Too often have I looked back over my shoulder,
   forgetful of your infinite desire to lead me on
   to the glory that lies ahead.

Lord God, how thankful I am
   that your are continually searching for me;
   how thankful I am
   that your grace prompts me to recognise you
   and to give myself to you even in my imperfect way.
Lord Jesus, how thankful I am
   that your love,
   stronger than death,
   will never let me go.
Holy Spirit, sweep me up into this love
   which unites you and the Father and the Son;
   let it flow into me
   and overflow from me to all whom I meet.
Let it lighten their darkness and increase their joy.
Let it draw me into unity with my brethren
   and with all those whom I serve
   and will serve in your name
   until the end of my days.

Glory and praise to you,
Father, Son and Holy Spirit, for ever.

*Alan Rees OSB (b. 1941)*

Lord, without you I can do nothing,       *199*
but with you, all things are possible.

200    Lord, since you exist, I exist;
        since you are beautiful, I am beautiful;
        since you are good, I am good.
    By my existence I honour you;
        by my beauty I glorify you;
        by my goodness I love you.
    Lord, through your power all things were made;
        through your wisdom all things are governed;
        through your grace all things are sustained.
    Give me power to serve you,
        wisdom to discern your laws,
        and grace to obey those at all times.

*Edmund of Abingdon (c.1180-1240)*

201    Most merciful God, order my day
        so that I may know what you want me to do,
        and then help me to do it.
    Let me not be elated by success or depressed by failure.
    I want only to take pleasure in what pleases you,
        and only to grieve at what displeases you.
    For the sake of your love,
        I would willingly forego all temporal comforts.
    May all the joys in which you have no part weary me.
    Let my thoughts frequently turn to you,
        that I may be obedient to you without complaint,
        patient without grumbling,
        cheerful without self-indulgence,
        contrite without dejection,
        and serious without austerity.
    Let me hold you in awe without being terrified of you,
        and let me be an example to others
        without any trace of pride.

*St. Thomas Aquinas (c. 1225-1274)*

Dear Lord, help me keep my eyes on you.        202
You are the incarnation of divine love;
   you are the expression of God's infinite compassion;
   you are the visible manifestation of the Father's holiness.
You are beauty, goodness, gentleness,
   forgiveness and mercy.
Outside you, nothing can be found.
Why should I look elsewhere?
You have the words of eternal life;
   you are food and drink;
   you are the Way, the Truth and the Life.
You are the light that shines in the darkness,
   the lamp on the lampstand,
   the house on the hilltop.
You are the perfection of God.
In and through you I can see and find my way
   to the heavenly Father.
O Holy One, Beautiful One, Glorious One,
   be my Lord and Saviour, my Redeemer,
   my Guide, my Consoler, my Comforter,
   my Hope, my Joy and my Peace.
To you I want to give all that I am.
Let me be generous, not stingy or hesitant.
Let me give you all
   – all I have, think, do and feel.
It is yours, O Lord.
Please accept it, and make it fully your own.

*Henri Nouwen (b.1932)*

Lord, make me your own,        203
until there is no lordship but yours in my life.

*Muslim Prayer*

204    O Lord, do not let me turn into a 'broken cistern'
        that can hold no water.
    Do not let me be so blinded by the enjoyment
        of the good things of earth
    that my heart becomes insensitive to the cry of the poor,
        of the sick, of orphaned children
        and of those innumerable brothers and sisters of mine
        who lack the necessary minimum to eat,
        to clothe their nakedness,
        and to gather their family together
        under one roof.

*Pope John XXIII (d. 1963)*

205    I unite and submit my will to yours
        in every event of this day
        however unpleasant,
        happy or boring.
    I will try not to be cast down by blame,
        failure, weakness and loneliness,
        nor elated by praise and success.
    Keep my soul in peace with you, Lord,
        and my body relaxed and free of tension.

*Alan Rees OSB (b. 1941)*

206    Lord, inspire me to read your scriptures
        and meditate upon them day and night.
    I beg you to give me real understanding of what I need,
        that I in turn may put its precepts into practice.
    Yet I know that understanding and good intentions
        are worthless unless rooted in your graceful love.
    So I ask that the words of scriptures
        may also be not just signs on a page
        but channels of grace into my heart.

*Origen (c.185-254)*

Gracious God, I praise and thank you         *207*
    that you have preserved me during the past week,
    and blessed the work of my hands.
Through each day
    you have helped me to build
    a temple of prayer in my heart,
    so that even in the midst of my labours
    I may rejoice in you.
And now on the day of rest
    I may devote all my attention to you.
Let the joy of this day
    be a foretaste of the joy of paradise.
Let this day of worship
    be a sign of the constant and everlasting worship
    around your heavenly throne.

Gracious God,
    help me this day to listen to your teachings,
    that my mind may be refashioned according to your love.
Let me turn a deaf ear to all idle and malicious gossip,
    and let me turn a blind eye to all temptation.
Make of me a new person,
    alert only to your truth,
    and alive only to your grace.
And thus let me celebrate Sunday after Sunday,
    and Sabbath after Sabbath,
    with unstinting devotion,
    until you shall admit me to the unceasing
    celebrations of heaven,
    the eternal Sabbath.

*Johann Starck (1680-1756)*

Teach me, O Lord, to do your will,         *208*
for you are my God.

209   Dear Lord, I will carry any cross you like,
          provided it is not my own.
      I find my own weaknesses so hard to bear;
          my own failure;
          my own depression.
      And yet, as well as I may, I offer my life to you.
      I ask you to bless it if you can,
          in ways I may never know.
      I ask you to use my failure, my breakdown,
          to help others in their quest for faith.
      Dear Lord, I offer my life and my failures to you,
          to be a blessing for others.
      Dear Lord, in your way and your time,
          please use me, for Jesus' sake.

*Graham Jeffery (b.1935)*

210   O Holy Spirit of God,
          take me as your disciple;
          guide me, enlighten me, sanctify me.
      Control my hands that they may do no evil,
          cover my eyes so that they may see it no more,
          and sanctify my heart so that evil may not dwell within me.
      Be my God; be my guide.
      Wherever you lead I will go;
          whatever you forbid I will renounce;
          and whatever you command me,
          in your strength I will do.
      Lead me, then, into the fullness of your truth.

*Henry E. Manning (1808-1892)*

# Prayers in
# Time of
# Trouble

*Peter was sad when Jesus asked him the third time: 'Do you love me?' He replied: 'Lord, you know everything.' (John 21:17)*

It is not easy repeating oneself, Lord, saying:        *211*
      'I love you,
      and I will follow you,'
      for the second and third,
      for the three hundredth time.
Yet we do it,
      as well as we can.
As a young man or woman first,
      more easily.
Then, when we are older
      and tied down to the world and life
      by a thousand little cords,
      we say again the old words:
      'Lord, you know that I am your friend.'
And though we say it with awkwardness,
      with rheumatism in our limbs
      and tiredness and lost opportunities in our hearts,
      still you hear us,
      and receive us,
      and lead us on.

*Graham Jeffery (b. 1935)*

Hold my hand, Lord,        *212*
   walk me through the loneliness
   and the valley of my sorrow.
Hold on to me when I'm too afraid
   to think about the future.
Let me lean on you, Lord,
   when I'm too weary to continue.
Hold my hand, Lord, through the night
   until I see the light of dawn.

*Author unknown*

213 Abba, Father,
  the world is quiet.
Everyone is asleep except me.
I worry about so many things.
Now I worry that I will still not have slept
  when it is time to get up.
Help me to relax,
  to put aside disturbing thoughts
  and think instead of your closeness to me.
In these moments of quiet
I ask for your Spirit,
the Spirit who brings peace and tranquillity,
  to enfold me in his love,
  removing all fear and anxiety,
  and instilling his calmness into
  the very centre
  of my being.

*Anthony Bullen*


214 I am tired, Lord,
  too tired to think,
  too tired to pray,
  too tired to do anything.
  Too tired.
Drained of resources,
  labouring at the oars against a head wind,
  pressed down by a force as strong as the sea.
Lord of all power and might,
  your way was through the sea,
  your path was through great waters,
calm my soul,
take control,
Lord of all power and might.

*Rex Chapman*

Lord Jesus,                                                             215
in your agony in the garden you said,
    'My soul is sorrowful
    to the point of death.'
I too am now feeling sad and despondent.
You know the cause.
The power of your Spirit can give me the remedy.
Heal me, Lord, of this depression.
Give me the joy and peace of knowing
    that nothing in my life or death
    can separate me from you.

*Author unknown*

Dear Lord,                                                             216
    you see the life I try to live
    within the life I live.
Beneath my fears,
    failures and inadequacies,
    you reach down and touch me.
You love me.
You are my friend.

*Graham Jeffery (b.1935)*

Lord Jesus Christ,                                                     217
    who very early in the morning
    while the sun was still rising,
    rose from the dead:
raise me up daily to newness of life,
    and save me,
    for you are my Lord and Saviour.

*Lancelot Andrewes (1555-1625)*

218   I give back to you, O God,
     one whom you first gave to me.
  You did not lose her *(him)* when you gave her to me,
    and I do not lose her by her return to you.
  Your Son has shown that life is eternal
    and love cannot die.
  So death is only a horizon,
    and a horizon is only the limit of our sight.
  Open my eyes to see more clearly,
    and draw me closer to you
     that I may know that I am nearer to my loved ones
    who are with you.
  You have promised that you are preparing a place for me;
    prepare me also for that happy place,
    that where you are I may also be,
    in your good time,
  O Lord of life and death.

*Bede Jarrett, OP*


*They made the grave secure; sealed with a stone, and guarded.*
*(Matthew 27:66)*

219   When all hope is gone, Lord,
    you are born.
  When the darkness is complete,
    you come.
  When things are beyond despair,
    I find you.
  You roll back the stone
    and are there to greet me.

*Graham Jeffery (b. 1935)*

O God my Father, bless and help me 220
   in the illness that has come upon me.
Give me courage and patience,
   endurance and cheerfulness
   to bear all weakness and all pain;
   and give me the mind at rest
   which will make my recovery all the quicker.
Give to all doctors, surgeons and nurses
   who attend me
   skill in their hands,
   wisdom in their minds,
   and gentleness and sympathy in their hearts.
Help me not to worry too much,
   but to leave myself in the hands
   of wise and skilful people
   who have the gift of healing,
   and in your hands.
Lord Jesus, come to me this day and at this time,
   and show me that your healing touch
   has never lost its ancient power.
This I ask for your love's sake.

*William Barclay (1907-1978)*

My Father, 221
   when I am inclined to panic,
   or to act hastily,
   help me to rest in the shadow of your love.
Keep me cool and calm
   in the heat of the world's busyness.
Give me the spirit of humility,
   and keep me from all harshness,
   intolerance and pride.
May I gladly use my strength
   to carry my neighbour's cross.

*J. H. Jowett (1864-1923)*

222   O God of peace,
      unite the hearts of all people
      that we may live with one another
      in gentleness and humility, in peace and unity.
O God of patience,
      give us patience in times of trouble,
      and courage to endure to the end.
O Spirit of prayer,
      awaken our hearts
      that we may lift up holy hands to God
      and cry to him in all our distress.
Be our defence in time of need,
      our help in trouble,
      our consolation when all things seem to be against us.
Come, eternal light, salvation and comfort;
      be our light in darkness,
      our salvation in life,
      our comfort in death,
      and lead us in the narrow way to everlasting life,
      that we may praise you for ever,
      through Jesus Christ our Lord.

*Bernard Albrecht (d.1636)*

223   Lord, I acknowledge my utter helplessness in this situation
      and my total dependence upon you.
I bring this problem to you with confidence,
      knowing that all things are possible with you.
Turn it to a means of good, not evil, for those involved,
      and by your love take the bitterness out of any
      painful circumstances or relationships,
      so that everything may be healed,
      reconciled and resolved through your power.

*Alan Rees OSB (b. 1941)*

*Each day has troubles enough of its own. (Matthew 6:34)*

Lord, I ask your blessing                    224
   on this moment only.
Nothing else.
The past is the past,
   though I often regret it.
Tomorrow will come,
   and I'm often afraid of it.
But this moment only
   can I influence in any way.
And I need your help
   to do it.

*Graham Jeffery (b. 1935)*


Give me your light, O Lord,                    225
   that the darkness of my heart may vanish away,
   and I may come to the true light,
   who is Jesus Christ my Lord.

*Author unknown*


Steer the ship of my life, good Lord,                    226
   to your quiet harbour where I can be safe
   from the storms of sin and conflict.
Show me the course I should take.
Renew in me the gift of discernment,
   so that I can always see the right direction
   in which I should go.
   and give me the strength and the courage
   to choose the right course,
   even when the sea is rough and the waves are high,
   knowing that by suffering hardship
   and danger in your name
   I shall find comfort and peace.

*St. Basil of Caesarea (c.330-379)*

227 Dear Lord, you know that the territorial instinct
    is for us humans the most basic instinct of all.
But what of us who have no territory,
    and no place to lay our head
    and call our own?
We are moved on.
We have no chance
    to develop and grow.
But our roots are in you, Lord;
    the one without territory,
    without space,
    who yet gives us space
    to be ourselves,
    and is our territory
    and home for ever.

*Graham Jeffery (b.1935)*

228 O eternal God,
    helper of the helpless,
    comforter of the comfortless,
    hope of the afflicted,
    bread of the hungry,
    drink of the thirsty,
    and saviour of all who wait upon you:
I bless and glorify your name;
I adore your goodness and delight in your love.
Take from me every tendency toward sin or vanity;
    let my desires soar upwards to your love,
    that I may hunger and thirst for the bread of life
    and the wine of heaven,
    and know no love but yours.

*Jeremy Taylor (1613-1667)*

Christ, give me strength;                                    *229*
    your servant is not well.
The tongue that praised you is made silent,
    struck dumb by the pain of sickness.
I cannot bear not to sing your praises.
O make me well again,
    make me whole,
    that I may again proclaim your greatness.
Do not forsake me, I beseech you.
Let me return now to your service.

*Gregory of Nazianzus (329-389)*

Lord, hear my voice when I cry to you!                       *230*
My heart says:
    I have longed,
    earnestly have I longed,
    to gaze upon your face.
Do not turn your face away from me.
Look tenderly upon your servant
    and, in your love,
    teach me to be free.

*Carmelite Monastery, Quidenham*

Lord, I am one of those on the ledge,                        *231*
    and the ledge gets narrower over the years.
It has never been very wide
    but I have managed to live there;
    managed to survive,
    managed to smile.

    My friends think I am doing rather well,
        things will somehow improve.
    but the ledge is getting smaller
        until I have nowhere to stand.
    Help me to cling on to your love,
        until I fall into your arms.

*Graham Jeffery (b.1935)*

232  Lord, look upon me with the eyes of your mercy.
     May your healing hand rest upon me;
          may your life-giving power
          flow into every cell of my body
          and into the depths of my soul,
          cleansing, purifying,
          restoring me to wholeness and strength
          for service in your kingdom.

*Author unknown*

233  Dear Lord,
          I am one of those people
          on the wrong side of life's road,
          as the people pass me by
          on the way to Jericho,
          on their way from the holy city.
     I try to make the journey
          but find it too much for me,
          half dead and half alive.
     I am only able to listen now and wait,
          as well as I may,
          for the sound of your donkey's footsteps.
     Please stop, Lord,
          as I know you always do.
     Stop, pick me up,
          carry me to safety.
     It is your journey, Lord;
          you make it with me.

*Graham Jeffery (b.1935)*

234  O God, the only source of health and healing,
     the spirit of calm and the central peace of this universe,
     grant me such a consciousness of your indwelling
     and surrounding presence that I may accept the health,
     strength and peace you are longing to give.

*Author unknown*

Lord, please tell me who I am.                                    235
I have changed job,
   been divorced,
   lost my house,
   lost any sense of identity or direction.
Yet you tell me who I am.
Only love can reach certain conditions:
   only you on your cross.
Love is the answer.
What was the question?

*Graham Jeffery (b.1935)*

O God, make haste to my rescue;                                  236
Lord, come to my aid.

*Psalm 69*

From all danger deliver me, O Lord.                              237

O Jesus, with all my heart I cling to you.                       238

Guard me as the apple of your eye.                               239
Hide me in the shadow of your wings.

*Psalm 16:8*

# Prayers for the World, Church & People

I bring before you, O Lord,          240
    the troubles and perils of people and nations,
    the pain of prisoners and captives,
    the sorrows of the bereaved,
    the needs of strangers,
    the vulnerability of the weak,
    the downheartedness of the weary,
    the diminishing powers of the aged.
O Lord, draw near to each,
    for the sake of Jesus Christ our Lord.

*St. Anselm (1033-1109)*

O God,          241
    the creative touch of beauty
    and the wellspring of love,
    blend in our lives the mysterious strength
    that radiates from you the Creator,
    the compassion of you the Son
    and the inspiration of you the Spirit.
May we invigorate the steps of the sad,
    lighten those gripped by darkness,
    and love the unloved and the hearts of stone,
    knowing always the assurance of the stillness
    and the strength of the love
    in Jesus Christ ever present.

*Martin Shaw*

Grant, O Lord,          242
    that none may love you less this day
    because of me;
    that no word or act of mine
    may turn one soul from you;
    and for one more grace I dare to pray,
    that many people may love you more this day
    because of me.

*Eric Milner-White (1884-1964)*

243   Almighty and most merciful Father,
      who has taught us not to think only of ourselves
      but also of the needs of others,
   I remember before you
      all who are burdened and oppressed,
      those whose hopes have been crushed
      and whose plans have come to nothing.

   I remember also
      those who are afflicted by poverty,
      or worn down by sickness and disease,
      those who are in darkness or despair,
      or who are suffering for righteousness' sake.

   Help them all, O God,
      to rest in you for comfort and strength.

*William Angus Knight (1836-1916)*

244   Loving Father,
      you have made all people in your likeness,
      and love all whom you have made.
   Let not the world separate itself from you
      by building barriers of race and colour.
   As your son was born of a Hebrew mother,
      yet rejoiced in the faith of a Syrian woman
      and a Roman soldier,
      welcomed the Greeks who sought after him
      and allowed a man from Africa to carry his cross,
      so teach all people to regard the members of all races
      as fellow heirs of your kingdom,
      through the same, Jesus Christ our Lord.

*Toc H Prayer*

Grant me grace, O Father,                                    245
not to pass by suffering or joy without eyes to see.
Give me understanding and sympathy,
and guard me from selfishness,
that I may enter into the joys and sufferings of others.
Use me to gladden and strengthen those
    who are weak or suffering;
that by my life I may help others to believe and serve you,
and shed forth your light which is the light of life.

*Dick Sheppard (1880-1937)*

Lord God, almighty creator,                                  246
teach me and all people to understand more and
    more profoundly that every human life is sacred,
whether it belongs to an unborn infant
or to a terminally-ill patient,
to a handicapped child
or to a disabled adult.

Remind us, heavenly Father,
that each individual has been made in your image and likeness
and has been redeemed by Christ.

Help us to see each other with your eyes,
so that we may reverence,
    preserve and sustain your gift of life in them
and use our own lives more faithfully in your service.

*Basil Hume (b. 1923)*

247   Dear Lord, are we ready to say it yet?
Not 'I believe in one God',
   which is easily said,
   the words tripping,
   appropriately, off our lips.
But your love asks us to go further.
Your love impels us to say:
   'I believe in one world.'

*Graham Jeffery (b.1935)*

248   O Lord and heavenly Father,
I commend to your care the people of this land
who are suffering distress and anxiety through lack of work.
Strengthen and support them, I pray;
and so increase the wisdom of those who direct our industries
that people may be set free from want and fear,
to work in peace and security for the relief of their necessities
and the well-being of the nation.

*Industrial Christian Fellowship*

249   Lord, shake away my indifference and insensitivity to the
   plight of the poor.
When I meet you hungry, thirsty or as a stranger,
show me how I can give you food,
   quench your thirst
   or receive you in my home
   – and in my heart.
Show me how I can serve you in the least of your brothers
   and sisters.

*Mother Teresa (b. 1910)*

Save your church, O Lord, from the fear of the truth,                    250
that it may not be found to work against you
    under the cloak of enthusiasm.

Make it ready to follow you along new paths
    when called to do so;
and grant that its knowledge of you be so strong and living
that it cannot help but sing to you a new song.

In all difficulties and troubles,
intensify in it that love which
    hopes all things,
    endures all things,
    and which never behaves inappropriately,
    but is always willing to be helpful.

*Herbert Morgan (1875-1946)*

O Lord, grant that I may not be conformed to the world          251
    but may love it and serve it.
Grant that I may never shrink from being
    an instrument of your peace
    because of the judgement of the world.
Grant that I may love you without fear of the world.
Grant that I may never believe that the inexpressible
    majesty of yourself
    may be found in any power of this earth.
May I firstly love you and my neighbour as myself.
May I remember the poor and the prisoner,
    the sick and the lonely,
    the young searchers,
    and those without homes,
    the lost and the fearful,
    as I remember Christ who is in them all.
And may I, this coming day,
    be able to do some work of peace for you.

*Alan Paton (1903-1988)*

252   Lord Jesus Christ, you are the way of peace.
Come into the brokenness of this world
   with your healing love.
Help us to be willing to bow before you in true repentance,
   and to bow to one another in real forgiveness.
By the fire of the Holy Spirit melt our hard hearts
   and consume the pride and prejudice
   which separate us from each other.
Fill us, O Lord, with your perfect love which casts out fear,
   and bind us together in that unity which you share
   with the Father and the Holy Spirit for ever.

*Cecil Kerr*

253   God of compassion,
   we acknowledge that you travel with those
   who have no resting place.
In your Son's flight into Egypt
   and in his helplessness,
   you took to yourself the heart of the refugee.
Love the forgotten ones who now long for a home but,
   through national and political upheaval, have none;
in Jesus Christ,
the lover of the lost ones,
our light and your love among us.

*Martin Shaw*

254   Make me worthy, Lord,
   to serve my fellow people throughout the world
   who die in poverty and hunger.
Give them through my hands this day their daily bread,
   and by my understanding love,
   give peace and joy.

*Mother Teresa (b.1910)*

Lord Jesus, when you were on earth,                                    *255*
   they brought the sick to you
   and you healed them all.
   Today I ask you to bless all those in sickness,
   in weakness and in pain;
   those who are blind and cannot see the light of the sun,
   the beauty of the world or the faces of their friends;
   those who are deaf and cannot hear the voices
   which speak to them;
   those who are immobile and confined to their homes.
Bless all such people.

   Those whose minds have lost their reason;
   those who are so nervous they cannot cope with life;
   those who worry about everything.
Bless all such people.

   Those whose weakness means they must always be careful;
   those whose disabilities mean that they cannot enter into
   the more strenuous activities or pleasures of life.
Bless all such people.

Grant that I in my health and my strength may never find those
   who are weak or disabled a nuisance,
   but grant that I may always do and give all that I can
   to see that they are included in the life of society.

*William Barclay (1907-1978)*


O God, the Father of all,                                              *256*
I commend to your ceaseless compassion
   all homeless children and orphans,
   and those whose lives are overshadowed by violence
   or thwarted by disease or cruelty.
Awaken in me your living love
   that I may not rest while children cry for bread
   or go uncomforted for lack of love.

*The Mothers' Union Service Book*

257   O loving Father,
     I pray for all who are disadvantaged on their journey of life;
       the blind,
        the sick in mind, body or spirit,
     and all who are disabled.
     I pray for those worn out with sickness
       and those who are wasted with unhappiness,
       for the dying and all unhappy children.
     May they learn the mystery of the road of suffering
       which Christ has trodden and the saints have followed,
       and bring you this gift which angels cannot bring:
       a heart that trusts you even in the dark.
     This I ask in the name of him who himself took
       our sorrows upon him,
       the same Jesus Christ.

*A. S. T. Fisher*


258   Open my eyes
     that they may see the deepest needs of men and women;
   Move my hands
     that they may feed the hungry;
   Touch my heart
     that it may bring warmth to the despairing;
   Teach me the generosity
     that welcomes strangers;
   Let me share my possessions
     to clothe the naked;
   Give me the care
     that strengthens the sick;
   Make me share in the quest
     to set the prisoners free;
   In sharing our anxiety and our love,
     our poverty and our prosperity,
     we partake of your divine presence.

*Canaan Banana*

Gracious Father, I pray for your holy, Christian church.  *259*
Fill it with all truth, in all truth with all peace.
 Where it is corrupt, cleanse it.
 Where it is in error, direct it.
 Where it is superstitious, rectify it.
 Where anything is amiss, reform it.
 Where it is right, strengthen and confirm it.
 Where it is in want, supply its need.
 Where it is divided and torn apart, heal the divisions,
 O Holy One of Israel.

*William Laud (1573-1645)*

Lord, I thank you for my family.  *260*
May we treat one another with respect, honesty and care.
May we share the little discoveries and changes each day brings.
May we always try to be sensitive to one another's joys, sorrows,
 needs and changing moods,
and realise that being a loving family means not necessarily
understanding everyone all the time,
but being there to love and help them just the same.

*Author unknown*

Be mindful of your church, O Lord.  *261*
 Deliver it from all evil,
 perfect it with your love,
 sanctify it,
 and gather it together from throughout the world
 into the kingdom which you have prepared for it.
For yours is the power and the glory for ever and ever.

*The Didache*

262 Guide and rule your church for ever, Lord,
       that it may walk warily in times of quiet
       and boldly in times of trouble;
       through our Lord Jesus Christ.

*Franciscan Breviary*

263 Look in mercy, heavenly Father,
       on this troubled and divided world.
   Though we cannot always trace your footsteps
       or understand your working,
       give us grace to trust you
       with an undoubting faith.
   And when the time you have set has come, Lord,
       show us the new heaven and the new earth,
       where righteousness lives
       and where the Prince of Peace rules,
       your Son, our Saviour Jesus Christ.

*Charles John Vaughan (1816-1897)*

264 Remember, O Lord, your church.
       Deliver it from evil and perfect it in your love.
       Strengthen and preserve it by your word and sacraments.
       Extend its influence,
       that your gospel may be preached to all nations.
   Gather the faithful from throughout the world
       into the kingdom which you have prepared.
       through Jesus Christ our Lord.

*Swedish Liturgy*

Lord,                                                 265
   the help of the helpless,
   the hope of those past hope,
   the rescuer of the storm-tossed,
   the harbour of the voyagers,
   the healer of the sick:
I ask you to become all things to all people,
   for you know the needs of each one.
Accept us all into your kingdom,
   making us children of light;
   and give us your peace and love,
   Lord our God.

*Liturgy of St. Basil (4th Century)*

Let the healing grace of your love, O Lord,            266
so transform me that I may play my part in the
   transfiguration of the world
from a place of suffering, death and corruption
to a realm of infinite light, joy and love.
Make me so obedient to your Spirit
that my life may become a living prayer,
and a witness to your unfailing presence.

*Martin Israel*

O God, who has bound us together in this bundle of life,    267
   give me grace to understand how all our lives depend
   on the courage, the work,
   the honesty and the integrity of others;
   so may I always be mindful of their needs,
   grateful for their faithfulness,
   and faithful in my responsibilities to them.

*Reinhold Niebuhr (1892-1971)*

268   Watch, dear Lord,
>    with those who wake, or watch, or weep tonight,
>    and give your angels charge over those who sleep.
> Tend your sick ones, O Lord Christ,
>    rest your weary ones,
>    bless your dying ones,
>    soothe your suffering ones,
>    pity your afflicted ones,
>    shield your joyous ones.
> I ask all this for your love's sake.

*St. Augustine of Hippo (354-430)*

269   Lord of the future, the only ruler in eternity,
>    set humankind free from the deadness of racial prejudice,
>    nationalism and greed for power over others;
>    enable the rich and powerful to find fulfilment
>    in caring for the poor and weak;
>    let the nations live together as one blood and fellowship,
>    for you are brother to all humankind
>    and by your blood we are set free from sin.

*Richard Garrard (b. 1937)*

270   Eternal God,
>    who through the passing years remain ever the same,
>    be near to all who are aged or infirm.
> Though their bodies fail,
>    let their spirits be strong in you,
>    that they may bear weariness and distress with patience and,
>    when their time comes,
>    may meet death unafraid,
>    through Jesus Christ our Lord.

*New Every Morning*

Give me, Lord God, a vision of the world                                    271
    as your love would make it:
a world where the weak are protected
    and none go hungry or poor;
a world where the benefits of civilised life
    are shared and everyone can enjoy them;
a world where different races, nations and cultures
    live in tolerance and mutual respect;
a world where peace is built with justice,
    and justice is guided by love;
and give me the inspiration and courage
to share in the task of building it,
through Jesus Christ my Lord.

*Author unknown*

O Lord,                                                                     272
our meal is steaming before us,
    and it smells very good.
The water is clear and fresh.
We are happy and satisfied.
But now we must think of our sisters
    and brothers all over the world
    who have nothing to eat
    and only a little to drink.
Please, please let them have enough to eat
    and enough to drink.
This is most important;
    but give them also
    what they need every day
    in order to get through this life.
Just as you gave enough to eat and drink
    to the people of Israel in the desert,
    please give it also
    to our hungry and thirsty brothers and sisters,
    now and at any time.

*An African Christian*

273    Lord Jesus, I praise and thank you
        that you have called and ordained servants
        within your church
        and set them apart for the ministry of word and sacrament.
    I pray that you will fill them with the fire of your love,
        that in their ministry they may be signs of
        your presence in the church.
    Since in themselves they are earthen vessels,
        I ask you to fill them with your power
        which shines in weakness.
    In sufferings, let them never be crushed;
        in doubt never despair;
        in temptation never be destroyed,
        in persecution never abandoned.
    Inspire them through prayer to live each day
        the mystery of your dying and rising.
    In times of weakness send them your Spirit,
        and help them to praise your heavenly Father
        and to pray for us.
    By your spirit, put your word on their lips
        and your love in their hearts,
        to bring good news to the poor
    and healing to the broken hearted.
    And pour out that same Spirit upon the church,
        that together we may be signs of your sacrificial love
        in the world, to the glory of God the Father.

*Author unknown*

274    My Father in heaven, I remember those
        whom in prayer I am inclined to forget.
    I pray for those whom I dislike.
    Defend me against my own feelings;
        change my inclinations;
        give me a compassionate heart.
    Give me, I pray, the purity of heart
        which finds your image in all people.

*J. H. Jowett (1864-1923)*

Lord, I pray for all humankind.          *275*
Although divided into nations and races,
   yet all people are your children,
   drawing from you our daily life and our very being,
   commanded by you to obey your laws
   in accordance with our knowledge and understanding.
Help us to overcome strife and hatred,
   that lasting peace may fill the earth
   and humanity everywhere be blessed with the fruit of peace.
So shall the spirit of unity among all people
   show forth our faith that you are the Father of all.

*Based on a Jewish Prayer*

Hear my humble prayer, O God, for all animals,          *276*
   especially those which are suffering:
   all that are overworked,
   underfed or otherwise cruelly treated;
   for all captive animals that long for freedom,
   and those that are hunted or lost,
   deserted, frightened or hungry.
I pray also for any creatures that are in pain or dying,
   and those that must be humanely destroyed out of kindness.
I ask that all who work with animals
   may have love in their hearts,
   gentleness in their hands
   and kind words on their lips.
Finally, help me to be kind and caring
   in all my dealings with animals
   and so to be an instrument of your compassion,
   for the sake of your Son who loves all creation,
   Jesus Christ my Lord.

*Based on a Russian prayer*

277   Father of all, hear me
when I pray for people of every race and nation.
May the light of your love break upon them,
lightening their burdens
and easing their anxieties.

Especially I pray for the marginalised
and the neglected.
May my vision, and the vision of others,
be increased that we become more aware
of forgotten and unwanted people.
Help us so to order our lives
and our societies
that no-one is excluded.

*Based on prayers by J. H. Jowett (1864-1923)*


278   Lord Jesus, poorest of the poor,
born in a borrowed stable
and buried in a borrowed tomb,
I bring before you all those who, like you,
have nowhere to lay their head:
the war refugees exiled from their homes,
migrants searching for a place to live,
the victims of earthquakes, floods and disasters,
and the countless, countless homeless in this land.
Help me, living as I am securely and in peace,
to show compassion for my brothers and sisters,
and to help them find in their lives
a new beginning and new hope,
for your name's sake.

*H. J. Richards (b. 1921)*

Eternal Father, 279
source of life and light,
whose love extends to all people,
all creatures, all things,
 grant me that reverence for life
 which becomes those who believe in you;
 lest I despise it, degrade it,
 or come callously to destroy it.
Rather, let me save it,
 secure it and sanctify it,
 after the example of your Son
Jesus Christ my Lord.

*Robert Runcie*


Lord Jesus, be near to all young children, 280
 that in the vulnerability and confusion,
 which this age can cause their growing personalities,
 they may come to no harm by the influence of adults;
 and grant to parents such sure knowledge of your love
 that they may guide their children with courage and faith.

*New Every Morning*


Lord, 281
I pray for all those whose lives have touched mine,
 for good or evil,
 in the past or in the present,
 whether they are alive or departed.
Give them an abundance of your grace in this world,
 and in eternity may they find joy in your presence,
 in the name of Jesus the Lord.

*Alan Rees OSB (b. 1941)*

282   Lord, make the old tolerant,
       the young sympathetic,
       the great humble,
       the busy patient.
Make rich people understanding
       strong people gentle,
       those who are weak prayerful.
Make the religious lovable,
       happy folk thoughtful,
       the clever kindly,
       the bad good,
       the good pleasant,
and, dear Lord,
       make me what I ought to be.

*Author unknown*

283   Give me the insight, Lord, to feel as others feel.
Give me the imagination to stand in another's shoes.
Your mercy is great because you know in Jesus
       what it is to be human.
Help me to share in this mercy.

*Rex Chapman*

284   Be pleased, O Lord, to remember my friends,
       all who have prayed for me,
       and all who have been good to me.
Do good to them,
       and return all their kindness twofold,
       rewarding them with blessings,
       sanctifying them with your grace,
       and bringing them to glory.

*Jeremy Taylor (1613-1667)*

O God, we are one with you.                    *285*
You have made us one with you.
You have taught us that if we are open to one another
    you dwell in us.
Help us to preserve this openness
    and to fight for it with all our hearts.
Help us to realise that there can be no understanding
    where there is mutual rejection.
O God, in accepting one another
wholeheartedly, fully, completely,
    we accept you,
    and we thank you,
    and we adore you,
    and we love you with our whole being,
    because our being is in your being,
    our spirit is rooted in your spirit.
Fill us then with love,
    and let us be bound together with love
    as we go our diverse ways united in this one spirit
    which makes you present in the world,
    and which makes you witness
    to the ultimate reality that is love.

Love has overcome.

Love is victorious.

*Thomas Merton (1915-1968)*


Father,                                        *286*
your own Son did not refuse to be born
    in the very thick of our muddle.
Humbly imitating him,
    may I show to your world
    the new life by which we are transformed.

*Carmelite Monastery, Quidenham*

287   Dear Lord, you have sent me into this world
     to preach your word.
So often the problems of the world seem
   so complex and intricate
   that your word strikes me as embarrassingly simple.
Many times I feel tongue-tied in the company of people
   who are dealing with the world's
   social and economic problems.

But you, O Lord, said, 'Be clever as serpents
   and innocent as doves'.
Let me retain innocence and simplicity
   in the midst of this complex world.
I realise that I have to be informed,
   that I have to study the many aspects of the
   problems facing the world,
   and that I have to try to understand as fully as possible
   the dynamics of our contemporary society.
But what really counts is that all this information,
   knowledge and insight
   allows me to speak your truthful word
   more clearly and unambiguously.
Do not allow evil powers to seduce me with the
   complexity of the world's problems,
   but give me the strength to think clearly,
   speak freely and act boldly in your service.
Give me the courage to show the dove
   in a world so full of serpents.

*Henri Nouwen (b.1932)*

288   Lord, open our eyes,
     that we may see you in our brothers and sisters.
Lord, open our ears,
     that we may hear the cries of the hungry,
     the cold, the frightened and the oppressed.

Lord, open our hearts,
 that we may love each other as you love us.
Renew in us your spirit,
Lord, free us and make us one.

*Mother Teresa (b. 1910)*

Strengthen me, Lord, to face the task,     *289*
 the crucifying task,
 of being a reconciler amongst guilt and fear,
 anxiety and anger.
Bring me, Lord, further to the point
 where I can accept life, with all its problems and pains,
 with gladness and exultation,
 not because of future perks in a future heaven,
 but because I know that to be fully human I can do no other.

*Rex Chapman*

You, O God, are the Lord of the mountains and valleys.     *290*
You are my mother and my father.
You have given me rain to make the corn grow,
 and sunshine to ripen it.
Now in your strength the harvest begins.

I offer you the first morsels of the harvest.
I know it is almost nothing compared with
 the abundance of the crop.
But since you have provided the harvest,
 my gift to you is only a sign of what you have given to me.

You alone know how many suns and moons
 it will take to finish reaping.
You alone know how heavy the crop will be.
If I work too hard and too fast
 I forget about you who gave me the harvest.
So I will work steadily and slowly,
 remembering that each ear of corn
 is a priceless gift from you.

*A Sioux prayer*

# Prayers of Blessing & Commendation

Into your hands, O Father and Lord,                     291
I commend my soul and body,
  my parents and home,
  my family, friends and neighbours,
  all people of faith and love,
  and all who stand in special need.
Lighten our lives with your holy grace
  and the knowledge of your constant presence,
O Lord in Trinity, God everlasting.

*St. Edmund of Abingdon (c.1175-1240)*


Deep peace of the running wave,                     292
deep peace of the flowing air,
deep peace of the quiet earth,
deep peace of the shining stars
deep peace of the Son of Peace,
  be with me for ever.

*Celtic Benediction*


May the peace of God,                     293
  which surpasses all understanding,
  keep my heart and mind
  in the knowledge and love of God,
  and of his Son, the Lord Jesus Christ:
and may the blessing of God almighty,
  Father, Son and Holy Spirit,
  be with me and all whom I love,
  now and always.

*Adapted from the Book of Common Prayer*

294    Take me to yourself, Lord,
        that I may truly live.
    I know that you will do all things for me;
        you will never disappoint me.

*Carmelite Monastery, Quidenham*

295    May the grace of the Lord Jesus Christ,
        the love of God
        and the fellowship of the Holy Spirit
    be with me evermore.

*Based on 2 Corinthians 13:13*

296    God be in my head, and in my understanding.
    God be in my eyes, and in my looking.
    God be in my mouth, and in my speaking.
    God be in my heart, and in my thinking.
    God be at my end, and at my departing.

*Book of Hours (1514)*

297    Lord Jesus Christ,
    I praise and thank you for those closest to me
        whom you have given to me to cherish.
    Surround them with your tender loving care,
        teach them to love and serve one another in true affection
        and to look to you in all their needs.
    I place them all in your care,
        knowing that your love for them is greater than my own.
    Keep us close to one another in this life
        and conduct us at the last to our true and heavenly home.
    Blessed be God for ever.

*Author unknown*

Holy God, I place myself in your hands.                    298
　　Bless me and care for me,
　　be gracious and loving to me;
　　look kindly upon me and give me peace.

*Based on the Aaronic blessing: Numbers 6:24-26*


God the Father, bless me;                    299
Jesus Christ, take care of me;
Holy Spirit, enlighten me all the days of my life.
O Lord, be my defender and keeper,
　　both now and for ever, through all ages.

*Aedelwald, Saxon Bishop, 9th Cent.*


O Lord my God, thank you                    300
　　for bringing this day to a close.
Thank you for giving me rest
　　in body and in soul.
Your hand has been over me
　　and has guarded and preserved me.
Forgive my lack of faith,
　　and any wrong that I have done today,
　　and help me to forgive all who have wronged me.
Let me sleep in peace under your protection,
　　and keep me from all the temptations of darkness.
Into your hands I commend my loved ones;
I commend to you my body and soul.
O God, may your holy name be praised.

*Dietrich Bonhoeffer (1906-1945)*


Into your hands I commend my spirit.                    301

*Psalm 30*

302   Bless me, God the Father,
        you who have created me.
      Bless me, God the Son,
        you who have set me free.
      Bless me, God the Holy Spirit,
        you who make me holy.
      O blessed Trinity, keep me in body,
        soul and spirit, to life eternal.

*'Weimarischer Gesangbuch' (1873)*


303   I commend to you, O God,
        my soul and my body,
        my mind and my thoughts,
        my prayers and my hopes,
        my health and my work,
        my life and my death,
        my relatives and my friends,
        my neighbours and fellow citizens,
        and all people,
        this day and always.

*Lancelot Andrewes (1555-1626)*


304   May the rich blessing of the Lord be with me,
        and forgive my sins.
      May the Lord graciously protect me from all evil
        and keep me in all good.
      May he who created and redeemed me
        keep me for himself without blemish to the end.

*Mozarabic Sacramentary (3rd Century)*

Father, I surrender myself into your hands;          *305*
  do with me what you will.
Whatever you may do,
  I accept with thanks.
  I am prepared.
Let your will alone be done in me
  and in all your creatures.
I wish no more than this, O Lord.

Into your hands I commend my soul.
I offer it to you with the love of all my heart,
  for I love you, Lord,
  and so need to give myself,
  to surrender myself into your hands without reserve,
  and with boundless confidence,
  for you are my Father

*Charles de Foucauld (1858-1916)*

May the strength of God lead me,          *306*
  may the power of God preserve me,
  may the wisdom of God instruct me,
  may the hand of God protect me,
  may the way of God direct me,
  may the shield of God defend me,
  may the hosts of God guard me
  against the snares of evil
  and the temptations of the world.
May your salvation, O Lord, always be mine
  this day and for evermore.

*St. Patrick (349-461)*

307    I surrender myself totally to you, Lord.
I renounce my own will and desires.
I accept the cross with praise and thanksgiving.
I will not fight you, Lord,
    nor the difficult people and circumstances
    that come my way.
I renounce all rebellion
    and place myself at the disposal
    of my brothers and sisters
    in trust and serenity.
I surrender myself totally to you, my Lord.

*Alan Rees OSB*

308    Bless your servant,
    with health of body and of spirit.
Let the hand of your blessing
    be upon her *(his)* head night and day,
    and support her in every need,
    strengthen her in temptations,
    comfort her in all sorrows,
    and let her be your servant in all circumstances;
    and help us both to live with you for ever in your favour,
    and in the light of your face,
    and in your glory.

*Jeremy Taylor (1613-1667)*

# Indices

# The Day at Prayer

**The beginning of the day**
1, 2, 3, 9, 11, 21, 24, 27, 35, 48, 50, 53, 57, 60, 62, 67, 77, 79, 83, 98, 102, 108, 111, 121, 122, 123, 124, 143, 156, 159, 163, 169, 170, 180, 181, 188, 201, 205, 217, 242, 251, 254, 255, 288, 293, 297, 304, 308

**At work**
3, 21, 27, 36, 37, 40, 44, 48, 50, 135, 161, 172, 174

**Encountering others**
3, 7, 18, 31, 34, 35, 36, 46, 48, 49, 62, 66, 67, 68, 77, 97, 102, 155, 161, 170, 180, 181, 251, 254, 308

**In relaxation**
27, 44, 50, 93, 132, 135, 137, 139, 140, 292

**Meal times**
58, 88, 104, 272

**The end of the day**
6, 11, 32, 76, 93, 101, 105, 106, 114, 125, 127, 130, 132, 140, 146, 213, 214, 216, 224, 225, 226, 232, 237, 239, 256, 268, 281, 284, 291, 292, 295, 296, 298, 299, 305, 307

# The Year at Prayer

**Advent**
4, 13, 17, 24, 252

**Christmas**
10, 25, 65, 104, 115, 128, 193, 202, 253, 256, 286

**Lent**
38, 41, 51, 54, 63, 76, 78, 91, 97, 113, 117, 118, 126, 129, 134, 135, 142, 144, 146, 155, 158, 160, 164, 171, 188, 192, 201, 250

**Passiontide**
26, 44, 73, 89, 91, 100, 103, 110, 113, 134, 148, 151, 154, 157, 209, 215, 219, 257, 289

**Easter**
115, 133, 145, 156, 163, 176, 189, 193, 211

**Pentecost**
2, 5, 16, 17, 98, 109, 149, 153, 162, 176, 259, 262, 264, 273, 275

**Harvest**
103, 104, 111, 249, 290

**One World Week**
7, 17, 34, 36, 43, 57, 66, 67, 73, 75, 76, 78, 80, 84, 86, 94, 144, 148, 151, 155, 157, 160, 165, 170, 171, 179, 180, 181, 188, 190, 193, 196, 204, 222, 227, 240, 243, 244, 248

**Week of prayer for Christian unity**
34, 43, 45, 72, 78, 87, 102, 113, 144, 155, 160, 176, 178, 181, 188, 196, 227, 250, 252, 259, 261, 262, 264, 283, 285, 289

**On holiday**
27, 49, 50, 53, 68, 69, 71, 75, 76, 81, 83, 84, 85, 86, 88, 93, 94, 140, 204, 226, 246, 247, 249, 251, 252, 253, 254, 255, 256, 258, 266, 267, 269, 271, 275, 277, 278, 279, 283, 287, 288, 289, 290

**Back to work/school**
3, 27, 36, 40, 44, 48, 50, 62, 77, 79, 99, 172, 179, 188, 201, 221, 248, 306

**Birthdays and anniversaries**
32, 34, 37, 38, 50, 64, 69, 81, 83, 85, 87, 88, 90, 104, 114, 156, 189, 191, 198, 200, 216, 226, 260, 280, 297, 308

**New Year**
2, 5, 21, 43, 271

**Sunday**
*Before worship*
6, 12, 13, 14, 15, 16, 20, 21, 26, 28, 30, 33, 52, 58, 60, 72, 137, 139, 169, 175, 177, 207, 228, 296

*After worship*
18, 19, 22, 39, 45, 59, 190, 197, 206, 291, 303, 306